The

HANGOVER HANDBOOK
and BEER LOVER'S BIBLE

Nic van Oudtshoorn

MAXIMEDIA

Maximedia is a registered trademark and imprint of
Maximedia Pty Ltd
PO Box 85
Jamberoo NSW 2533
Australia
Website: www.maximedia.com.au
Email: info@maximedia.com.au

ISBN: 978-1-921373-28-2

DISCLAIMER
The contents of this book is not to be taken internally.
This is a work of humour, not of medicine.
The author and publisher accept no liability for the efficacy or safety
of any of the recipes or "cures" described herein.
They are neither recommended or prescribed.

While every effort has been made to ensure that this book is free
from error or omissions, the publisher, author, and their respective
employees or agents shall not accept responsibility for injury, loss or
damage occasioned by any person acting or refraining from action
as a result of material in this book, whether or not such injury, loss
or damage is in any way due to any negligent act or omission,
breach of duty or default on the part of the publisher, author, or their
respective employees or agents.

Cartoons: Shane Summerton

PLEASE DRINK RESPONSIBLY AND DO NOT DRIVE AFTER DRINKING

Contents

HANGOVER AT WORK.

What is a hangover?

The dictionary defines a hangover as "the after effects of excessive indulgence in alcoholic drink". But that, as any sufferer will testify, is most inadequate to describe the agonies you suffer after the joys of the night before: Vesuvius erupting in your stomach, a bass drummer thumping on your brain, and a canary fouling its nest in your throat.

Here's a much better definition, supplied by a seasoned sufferer: *You've got a hangover if, after a heavy night on the tiles, you hear the cat walking across the carpet, forcing you to yell out: "Do you have to wake me by stamping your feet?"*

Is a hangover physical or mental? A University of Oklahoma professor, Dr Stewart Wolf, did an experiment to find out and came up with amazing results.

STOMP! STOMP! STOMP! STOMP! STOMP! STOMP!

He fed a group of human guinea pigs with clear consciences (they were told they were drinking in the interests of science) the same amount of grog as another group of ordinary drinkers were downing at a nearby pub. The aim of all of them was to get drunk — and, with the good professor footing the booze bill, they all did just that.

But, Dr Wolf reported later, not one of those who got smashed in the laboratory reported a hangover, while those who drank where they always drink woke up with throbbing heads, aching guts, horrible mouths and so on.

So what does that prove, you may ask. Well, concluded Dr Wolf, a hangover is nothing more than the showing of a person's guilt complex for getting drunk in the first place!

His theory is supported by other authorities. Explains Timothy Coffey, editor of the *Journal on Alcohol Studies*, "Come morning you are going to feel guilty about hanging one on. Guilt feelings about anything can give jitters and aches. So go ahead and concoct some foul-smelling remedy. It's a good way of punishing yourself and thereby relieving the guilt."

You'll be pleased to know you're not the only one suffering today. After extensive research, a Michigan University professor has now proved conclusively that pigs who drink too much suffer hangovers just like humans.

He is now trying to discover the perfect hangover cure for pigs, which he claims should work on humans as well.

As proof , the professor cites humorist Henry Morton's saying: "One drink of wine, and you act like a monkey; two drinks and you strut like a peacock; three drinks and you roar like a lion; and four drinks — you behave like a pig."

No respectable drinker will agree with that — so in the pages that follow you'll find distinctly human hangover recipes developed over the ages and in many countries.

There are so many, and their origins are often so obscure, that it has proved impossible in most cases to acknowledge the inventors.

The author and publisher can only say: "Thank you for your service to suffering humanity — we'll toast you all with our next drink!"

How do you tell a stinking hangover from an ordinary hangover? If you feel so sick you're afraid you're going to die, you're suffering a pretty ordinary hangover. It's only a real stinker when you become terrified that you'll stay alive — to continue suffering.

When I was two years of age she asked me not to drink, and then I made a resolution of total abstinence. That I have adhered to it and enjoyed the beneficent effects of it through all time, I owe by my grandmother. I have never drunk a drop from that day to this of any kind of water.

— MARK TWAIN

101 ways to cure that hangover

Mrs Theo. P. Winning's *Household Manual*, a medical bible for housewives a century ago, contains scores of old wives' remedies. To relieve a severe hangover headache, she advises, soak the feet in mustard and water until the headache vanishes.

Pepys' Breakfast Cure

Famous English diarist Samuel Pepys (pronounced "Peeps") had a boozy breakfast cure for hangovers, such as the one he served his suffering guests on New Year's morning 1661:

"A barrel of oysters, a dish of neats' tongues, a dish of

anchovies, wine of all sorts and Northdowne Ale."

Cool, Baby, Cool!

Cut up an unpeeled cucumber into small pieces, then sprinkle with two teaspoons of salt. Drink several spoonfuls of the resulting liquid.

Pommy Hot Dog

Juice of two lemons

1 teaspoon mustard powder.

Mix the mustard with the lemon juice and drink in one hit.

Bushman's Corny Cure

An old Australian recipe from the makers of bush tucker:

Mix cornflower with buttermilk in a pot, then heat until almost boiling point. Season with salt and pepper to taste.

Bitter Bubbly

Pour ice-cold champagne into a chilled glass, add one teaspoon of cognac and a dash of Angostura bitters, stir and drink.

Muscle Magic

Kingsley Amis offers this off-beat cure for even the most severe hangovers:

"Upon awakening, if your wife or other partner is beside you, and (of course) willing, perform the sexual act as vigorously as you can. The exercise will do you good and you'll feel toned up emotionally."

Roman bouncer

Roman drinkers believed prevention was better than cure so they regularly left the banquet hall to drink a glass or two of sea water and to be sick.

Then they bounced back to the wine ... and the party continued.

Royal Peter

Peter the Great of Russia swore that the only good hangover cure was warm brandy liberally spiced with pepper.

Suffering Bastard

Attributed to a barman at Cairo's old Shepheard Hotel, this hangover cure calls for:

Brandy

Lime Juice

Gin

Take one-third of each. Add dash of bitters. Mix with ginger ale. Sip slowly.

Dying Bastard

As for Suffering Bastard, but add a shot of Bourbon.

Dead Bastard

As for Dying Bastard, but add a shot of rum.

Dairy Delight

One nip vodka

Two nips tomato juice

Slug of Worcestershire sauce

Two Alka-Selzers

"A good squirt of cow's milk", preferably from the udder (full-cream milk from the milk bottle will do in an emergency).

Mix together, allowing the milk from the udder to foam up in the glass, or if from the bottle stir rapidly to get the same effect. Drink slowly.

Foaming Blood

Take a beer glass, fill it halfway with tomato juice, then top it up with beer.

Hot 'n Cold

Sitting with an ice-pack on your head and your feet in hot water "takes the blood from the brain", say some people, who claim it relieves the throbbing head and many other hangover symptoms.

Distilled dynamite

In a whisky tumbler, mix half a teaspoon of sugar with a dash of Angostura bitters. Add 1.5 nips of rye whiskey and one ice cube. Fill the glass with chilled champagne, then add two dashes of absinthe. Drink.

Prairie oyster

Drop a raw egg in a tumbler, season with salt and vinegar, Worcestershire or hot sauce. Then

Shut eyes, open mouth,
Murmur prayers for the soul,
Pop in and swallow whole ...

Tiger's Milk

(An authentic Thai hangover cure)
45ml of Baccardi
45ml of Cognac
Half cup of cream
Half cup of milk

Shake vigorously with ice, pour into a glass and flavour gently with nutmeg.

Virgin Mary

Mix one can of tomato juice with half a cup of lemon juice, salt and pepper and a celery stick. Drink.

Polish Bison

Attributed to author Kingsley Amis, this hangover cure requires you to mix a generous slug of vodka with a large teaspoon of Bovril beef extract, two tablespoons of lemon juice, water and pepper. Drink quickly.

Singapore Sling

To mix this great Oriental hangover cure, you need:

Juice of quarter lemon or 1 large lime

1 nip of cherry brandy

1.5 nips of gin

1 teaspoon sugar syrup

Dash of Angostura bitters.

Shake and strain into highball glass with one ice cube. Fill glass with ginger ale. Serve with slice of lemon peel.

Bloody Mary

Mix one part vodka with two to six parts tomato juice (the amount of tomato juice is determined by the ferocity of your hangover). Add dash of Worcestershire sauce. Serve with very thin slice of lemon floating on top.

Cures Around The World

Norway: A glass of heavy cream to settle the rebellious stomach.

Switzerland: Brandy with a dash of peppermint.

Russia: Cucumber juice, heavily salted. In some parts they also eat black bread soaked in water for breakfast.

Outer Mongolia: Pickled sheep's eye in tomato juice.

Germany: Sour herring with a beer chaser (or three). Sometimes the herring is combined with raw onions, sour cream or yoghurt.

Puerto Rico: Rub half a lemon under your drinking arm.

France: Thick black hot onion soup for breakfast.

Owl's That?

Pliny the Elder, a famous Roman, swore by Jupiter that the only morning-after cure was six raw owls' eggs swallowed in quick succession.

Swallow That!

In ancient Assyria, ground swallow beaks mixed with bitter myrrh was a prime recipe for a hangover.

Morning Glory Fizz

Juice of half a lime
Juice of half a lemon
1 egg white
2 teaspoons sugar syrup
1 pony of absinthe
1 jigger of Scotch

Shake together with crushed ice, strain into a large glass and top up with equal amount of soda water. (From David Embury's *The Fine Art of Mixing Drinks*)

Black Velvet

Pour half a Guinness into a glass, top up with an extra-dry champagne. Sip slowly. Repeat if necessary.

Extraordinary Bloody Mary

Attributed to Aussie chef extraordinaire Bernard King, it is made as follows:

Plug up your ears, then crush ice cubes in the blender. Half-fill a large glass with the crushed ice, packing tightly.

Add a good slug of vodka, topped with tomato puree, dashes of celery salt, Tabasco sauce, garlic salt and celery seed. Stir briskly. Drink slowly.

Remove the ear plugs and face the world.

Scots Guts

Two nips of whisky
One nip of Fernet Branca
Three dashes of Pernod
Pinch of salt
Dash of Tabasco

Mix together. Stir gently. Add ice and strain into a tall glass.

Cayenne Fizz

Take a half-litre of champagne, sprinkle with cayenne pepper, drink slowly.

Glorious Morning

This hangover cure consists of a measure of Fernet Branca and a dash of peppermint. Swallow very fast.

A Vitamin, I See

Vitamin C can not only cure hangovers, it can also sober up a dead drunk, an Australian doctor has found.

He says large doses of Vitamin C (between five and 30gm), taken very quickly, makes a hangover disappear rapidly. And it does not matter whether you take the tablets before or after you drink.

"Results are very dramatic," he reports. "Patients come in drunk with very high blood alcohol levels. Some are noisy, aggressive and hard to deal with. Others are dead drunk and unconscious or having fits.

"I give them 30gm of vitamin C in a solution intravenously, slowly over 10 or 20 minutes. Within minutes the fits stop, they sober up, lose their belligerence and become easier to handle. Some fall into a deep sleep lasting up to three hours and then wake up feeling normal."

His treatment has the support of Nobel prize-winner Dr Linus Pauling, who agrees a massive dose of vitamin C is the best way to cure a hangover.

Tart Eggs

Mix together vinegar and raw eggs — then gulp down in one hit.

The Jules Reviver

This hair-of -the-dog hangover cures comes from the famous Jules Bar, in Jermyn Street, London:

Pimms No 1 with a dash of Grand Marnier, topped with chilled champagne.

Heart Starter

A double gin, mixed with water and liver salts, then gulped down quickly for maximum effect.

Expense Account Cures

Hangover cures collected by the US financial newspaper *The Wall Street Journal*, for readers who know all about expense account drinking:

- ✿ A huge slug of **bitters** in a cold beer.
- ✿ A few whiffs of pure **oxygen**.
- ✿ **Buttermilk** heavily spiced with salt and pepper.
- ✿ Chewing wild **lettuce** leaves.
- ✿ A cup of plain **yoghurt**.
- ✿ A cup of **cherry-leaf tea** (no milk or sugar).

Slippery Slime

In the Middle Ages, a popular hangover remedy was a mixture of bitter almonds and raw eel.

Brown Bubbly

French wine producers met with a mixed response when they invited more than 200 doctors to a wine cellar — to try out a champagne-and-cognac hangover cure.

The mixture of one part cognac to three parts of champagne was pronounced "not a bad drop" by members of the Physicians Wine Appreciation Society of New York. But not one medico was willing to hail it as the perfect hangover remedy.

Dr Twinkle's Hangover Tonic

2-3 slices of cucumber
Few sprigs of parsley
Stick of celery
Lemon rind
2 grapes
3 tablespoons sugar
Dash vanilla essence

Liquidise, then pour into the first glass. This is the main drink.

Next, mix together:

Half a cup of milk
1 teaspoon Creme de Cacao
3 tablespoons cream
Pinch of salt
1 teaspoon sugar
Dash of bitters
1 teaspoon wheat germ

Beat in two eggs, then pour into the second glass.

Drink contents of glass one, followed quickly by the contents of glass two.

Royal Prunier

Said to be the Queen's favourite hangover cure, this remedy consists of four ounces of champagne mixed with four ounces of orange juice over ice.

Wooster Booster

Put a raw egg, yolk unbroken, into a cup with liberal

quantities of Worcestershire sauce. For speedy relief, gulp the mixture in one go, making sure the egg does not break until it reaches the back of your throat. That is claimed to take away the nausea.

Brandy Branca

Attributed to wine expert Len Evans, this hangover cure tastes horrible but is said to work wonders:

One ounce of brandy

Dash of Fernet Branca

Mix together and drink.

Hangover Casserole

To make this nasty concoction, reports Clement Freud, you:

Slice very thinly half a kilo of onions, simmer in 250gm of butter until soft, then pour a bottle of champagne into the pan. Decant the mixture in a soup tureen, cover with a layer of Camembert cheese and sprinkle toasted breadcrumbs on top. Bake in a medium oven until the cheese melts and the crumbs have been crisped.

Eat for breakfast after seasoning with black pepper.

Herring delight

12 salted herrings

250ml cider vinegar

3 Juniper berries

cloves

peppercorns

dash of water

Blend together. Drink slowly for breakfast.

007's Licence to Cure

James Bond (in *Thunderball* and *Moonraker*) uses this hangover cure:

Two aspirin taken with a glass of fruit salts — and plenty of pretty women on whom to feast those blood-shot eyes until they recover their usual lustful sparkle.

Highland Honey

Take one ounce of Scotch, one ounce of cream, and half an ounce of honey. Shake heavily in a cocktail shaker and add to shaved ice in a cocktail glass. Drink immediately.

Hart's Cure

Patented by Englishman Nathan Hart in 1904, this cure for everything from hangovers to consumption is easy to make but not that easy to swallow. You mix two garlic bulbs with a bottle of prime brandy, then warm the mixture slowly for a week before drinking.

You are what you eat

Eating before going out on a junket helps you drink more before you get drunk because it slows down the rate at which the stomach absorbs alcohol.

Some people also claim going on a binge on a full stomach reduces the agony of the hangover that follows.

A pre-drinking meal recommended by a doctor regarded as a world authority on hangovers:

Eat a bowl of milk and cornflakes (packed with vitamin

B) and an orange of two (for its vitamin C), followed by a plateful of potatoes, well salted and mashed with butter.

Some doctors say eating a breakfast of milk and steak is just the thing for hangover belly aches and nausea, with a couple of aspirin to settle the headache.

The Scots swear that hot porridge for breakfast is the best treatment for a hangover, particularly one induced by scotch.

STOP! COMPULSORY DRINK BREAK! It's time to have a drink and find out if you're sober enough to continue reading the hangover cures. Check the eye-chart and answer questions on the following pages — if you pass the test, turn to Page 28.

EYE

TEST TO

CHECK IF I

AM MUCH TOO

DRUNK TO READ

HOW TO PREVENT

A HANGOVER KILLING

ME TOMORROW MORNING

26

HOW DRUNK AM I?

TEST 1

Study the chart opposite, then answer the question: On what line does the word "tomorrow" appear? *(Hint: It is not near the top.)*

TEST 2

Study the pictures below and select whether A or B best reflects part of the treatment at the world's first Hangover Clinic? *(Hint: Page 60.)*

A

B

TEST 3

Solve this ridde: A man spends every night drinking, but never has a drop during the day. He drinks and drinks but never gets a hangover. His drink is always warm and comes straight from the source. What is it? *(Hint: He cannot survive without it.)*

Answers

1. Last line. 2. B. 3. A vampire drinking blood.

"I say, old chap ..."

A British doctor claims the best hangover cure is a tall glass of lemon juice and fructose mixed together.

Bees' Knees

8 parts gin

1 part honey

2 parts lemon juice

Shake with cracked ice. Strain and add two parts of orange juice. Drink.

Dry Gunpowder

One-third dry vermouth

One third Pernod

One-third brandy.

Stir well and serve.

Egg Burp

Pour half a bottle of beer into a short glass. Mix in one raw egg, stir until foam subsides.

Apple Banger

1 nip apple brandy

1 nip Dubonnet

Dash Angostura bitters.

Stir well with ice, strain into glass.

Pony Express

1 nip brandy

2 nips of port

Quarter teaspoon sugar

1 egg yolk

Stir and drink gently.

Brandy Pick-Up

2 nips brandy

White of 1 egg

Freshly squeezed juice of 1 lemon

Teaspoon caster sugar

Shake well, strain in to tall glass, fill with soda water.

Captain Blood

4 nips Bundaberg rum

1 nip lime juice

2 dashes bitters

Stir quickly and serve neat or over ice if preferred.

Pepper Pow-Wow!

1 nip Scotch Whisky

Juice of half a lemon

1 teaspoon Worcestershire sauce

1 teaspoon Chili sauce

1 dash Tabasco sauce

3 dashes bitters.

Stir well.

Spiced Soda

Pour warmed-up soda water into a tall glass. Add liberal dash of bitters. Drink as fast as possible.

Swiss Belly Blaster

1 part Vermouth

2 parts absinthe

Half teaspoon sugar syrup

1 egg white

Shake well with ice. Pour into tall glass (with the ice) and top up with soda water.

Water Torture

Before going to bed, drink half a litre of lightly salted water and two aspirin. Continue drinking the lightly-salted water every time you wake up during the night to restore the fluid balance.

Alcohol dehydrates the body and many experts believe this is a major cause of hangovers.

Sugar 'n Spice

Sugary soft drinks with plenty of fizz for breakfast is regarded as an excellent hangover cure by many sufferers. To turn it into a true "hair-of -the-dog", add a nip of rum or brandy.

Cliffhanger

Favourite of the fictional private eye Cliff Hardy, this cure consists of cask white wine diluted with soda water. Increase the concentration of the wine until the hangover vanishes.

Green Gratitude

Pour a generous jigger creme de menthe into a tall glass, then top up with soda water.

Blood 'n Guts

Flagellation to draw plenty of blood was the ancient Greek way to cure a hangover — when anyone was bold enough to admit having one, that is!

Jamaican Eyeball Plucker

1 nip overproof rum

1 teaspoon cream

1 teaspoon honey

Shake well with ice. Strain into glass.

Foaming brekky

Many serious drinkers, particularly in Australia and Germany, believe implicitly that the best morning-after cure is a few glasses of beer for breakfast. For speedier relief — and depending on the state of your stomach lining — add Angostura bitters to the beer. Others say flat beer is even better, so leave a can or two open before going to bed.

Stone the crows ... er, hangovers

Ancient Greeks believed Amethyst would protect them against hangovers, so they placed the precious stones in the bottom of their drinking vessels or embedded them in the side of their goblets.

Food for thought

Through the ages, many self-proclaimed hangover experts have advocated chewing your way health and happiness. Here are some of their suggestions:

☺ Slowly chew raw **root ginger**.

☺ Hot **bacon rolls** dripping with fat.

☺ "Greasy spoon" **hamburger** with lashings of ketchup, washed down with tomato juice.

☺ **Sauerkraut** and juicy sausages.

☺ Chinese **spring rolls**.

☺ **Grapefruit**.

☺ Dry **toast**.

A cabbage a day...

Keeping sober while drinking great quantities of wine — and avoiding a hangover — was a problem for the old Egyptians, until they discovered boiled cabbage!

A visitor to Egypt reported that "they are the only people amongst whom it is a custom at their feasts to eat boiled cabbages before all the rest of their foods — and even to this very time they do so, and many people add cabbage seeds to potions which they prepare as preventives against drunkenness and suffering the next day".

Cabbages also helped prevent hangovers, the old Romans believed — so much so they wrote a poem about its restorative values:

Last evening you were drinking deep,
So now your head aches. Go to sleep:
Take some boiled cabbage when you wake,
And there's an end to your headache!

— Quoted in *A Toast: Your Health!* by D.L. Ziegler.

Dr Jones' Honey Humdinger

Immediately after waking, force down six teaspoonfuls of honey every 20 minutes for the first hour. After three hours, repeat the treatment, then eat a soft-boiled egg.

Jumping Jackrabbit

This old Wild West cure, from the days when bad whiskey was served in tough saloons, treated many a gun-slinger's hangover. It's a treatment for those who suffer hangovers often enough to take precautions well in advance.

The recipe calls for "plenty of droppings from a jackrabbit", which should be well dried. You mix the dried dung into a strong tea with hot water, strain and drink every 30 minutes.

Bushies Delight

Australian boozers seeking a cure a century or so ago were given the following advice:

"Put half an ounce of ground quassia into one pint of good strong vinegar. Let it stand for 24 hours, then bottle, and every time a hangover strikes take two tea-spoonfuls in a little water and drink it down. The pain will gradually leave, but have it close at hand so there need be no excuse to suffer so much from the whisky again."

Make up your mind!

The tranquilliser Librium cures hangovers and sobers up drinkers twice as fast as coffee, a Swedish scientist told the 28th International Congress on Alcohol and Alcoholism. Dr Leonard Goldberg tested more than 1000 pie-eyed volunteers to reach that conclusion.

But before you rush off to your friendly doctor for a Librium prescription, here's the bad news. A Sydney University research team has reported that the effects of alcohol were considerably increased if the drinker was taking either Librium or another tranquilliser, Valium.

On the Trot

One popular cure for hangovers in the Low Counties of Holland is a trotter-and-liver soup. You boil sheep's trotters, cow's livers and oatmeal for six hours, then strain and eat the soup while hot.

Voodoo Corker

In Haiti, voodoo extends even to hangovers. An instant cure is produced, say locals, when you stick 13 black-headed pins in the cork of the bottle that gave you the hangover.

Grey Guts

Nineteenth-century chimney-sweeps swore by this hangover cure: Warm a cup of milk, then gently mix in a level teaspoonful of fine soot (soot created by burning hardwood is the best). Drink slowly. Repeat after 30 minutes if you are still feeling a bit off.

Adriatic Boot

Baume de Floriani, a mixture of Chianti, turpentine and a wide range of spices, was a popular hangover cure in Italy last century.

Kamikaze cure?

The Japanese cure a hangover by wearing a gauze surgical mask soaked in saki.

Bitter and Twisted

Two nips of good-quality cider vinegar — not cider — is a favourite way to cure hangovers in the west of England. And no wonder — they have lots of apple trees there and make cider for much of the country.

Devil's Delight

Take one cup of milk, mix in two tablespoons of castor oil, and warm the mixture until lukewarm. Season with red cayenne pepper. Sip slowly while still warm.

Toasted Red Indian

Burnt toast soaked in milk, then eaten with a spoon like porridge, is said to work wonders on a hangover, particularly one caused by red wine.

Greasy spoon walk

Aussie artist and hangover veteran Mark Elder offers the following advice:

"Lots of oxygen and greasy food work wonders in fighting hangovers. So, instead of taking a cab home from the pub, walk at least part of the way — and use the money you save to buy the greasiest hamburger with 'the lot' to keep you company. It works every time."

There is one qualification though — you need to be sober enough to find your way home!

Genghis Khan's cure

1 teaspoon Epsom salts

1 teaspoon cream of tartar

1 teaspoon ground ginger

Mix together, then dissolve one or more teaspoons in a glass of water and drink.

Let it all hang out!

If all else fails and spewing is the only solution, you can make a very fast-acting emetic by mixing mustard powder with water. Swallow fast ... then run!

Alcohol is the anaesthesia by which we endure the operation of life.

— GEORGE BERNARD SHAW

"Only Irish coffee provides in a single glass all four essential food groups: alcohol, caffeine, sugar and fat."

— TOM WATTS

AS CHURCHILL SAID ...

Field Marshal Bernard Montgomery primly told Sir Winston Churchill: "I do not smoke or drink and I am one-hundred per cent fit."

Churchill, who confessed he survived World War II on "cigars, brandy and crisis", calmly puffed his cigar, sipped his brandy and replied: "I smoke and drink — and I am two-hundred per cent fit!"

When a stout Labour MP, Bessie Braddock, accused Churchill of being drunk, he retorted: "And you, madam, are ugly, but tomorrow, I shall be sober."

Always remember, I have token more out of alcohol than alcohol has token out of me.

My rule of life prescribed as an absolutely sacred rite smoking cigars and also the drinking of alcohol before, after and if need be during all meals and in the intervals between them.

Meeting Franklin Roosevelt was like opening your first bottle of champagne; knowing him was like drinking it.

I have been brought up and trained to have the utmost contempt for people who get drunk.

One does not leave a convivial party before closing time.

What's behind a hangover?

"Water is best," Pindar, a Greek poet and wowser, said piously 2500 years ago. Of course, we all know that's not true, but we also have to admit that water does not make you drunk or give one a hangover.

So what is a hangover? There are almost as many theories as there are medical scientists, but generally they agree that is a combination of several of the following:

🌑 Too little fluid in the body, or dehydration.

🌑 Too much fluid in the brain.

🌑 A chemical created by alcohol that produces side effects.

🌑 Too much lactic acid in the stomach.

🌑 Too much carbon dioxide in the blood.

Drinking toasts started in ancient times as a way to improve the taste of wines.

Drinkers each soaked a piece of spiced toast in their cup, then ate it before draining the wine and wishing their fellow drinkers good health (probably because the wine often tasted like poison).

Shakespeare refers to this tradition in *The Merry Wives of Windsor*: "Go fetch me a quart of sack (wine), put a toast in't."

What causes the terrible suffering?

As a rule of thumb, the darker the drink, the worse the hangover. Thus you'll do best to drink white spirits and still white wines, rather than nipping into the brandy, sherry, red wine, or dark rum.

Sparkling wines of any colour, such as champagne, have more acids, which also increase the severity of a hangover. They also make you drunk more quickly, because the bubbles help the body to absorb the alcohol at an increased rate.

It's the alcohol in the booze that makes you drunk, but that is absorbed by the body pretty quickly. The main cause of a hangover is not alcohol as such, but dirty little demons called congeners (impurities) that lurk inside every kind of booze.

Congeners are mostly chemical by-products of fermentation and maturing processes and give the distinctive flavour and characteristics to "natural" wines, spirits and beers. More than 100 congeners have so far been identified.

The amount of impurities in various drinks should warn you how lethal are the hangovers they cause.

One scientific way to check this theory is to partake of sufficient quantities of various drinks — a different one each night — to give you a hangover. You can then compare the ferocity of the headache, nausea and so on of each.

A much easier way is to turn the page and consult the *HANGOVER SEVERITY CHART*, which is based on scientific research and hard-earned human experience through the ages.

HOW TO PICK YOUR

⇩ *HANGOVER SEVERITY RATING*

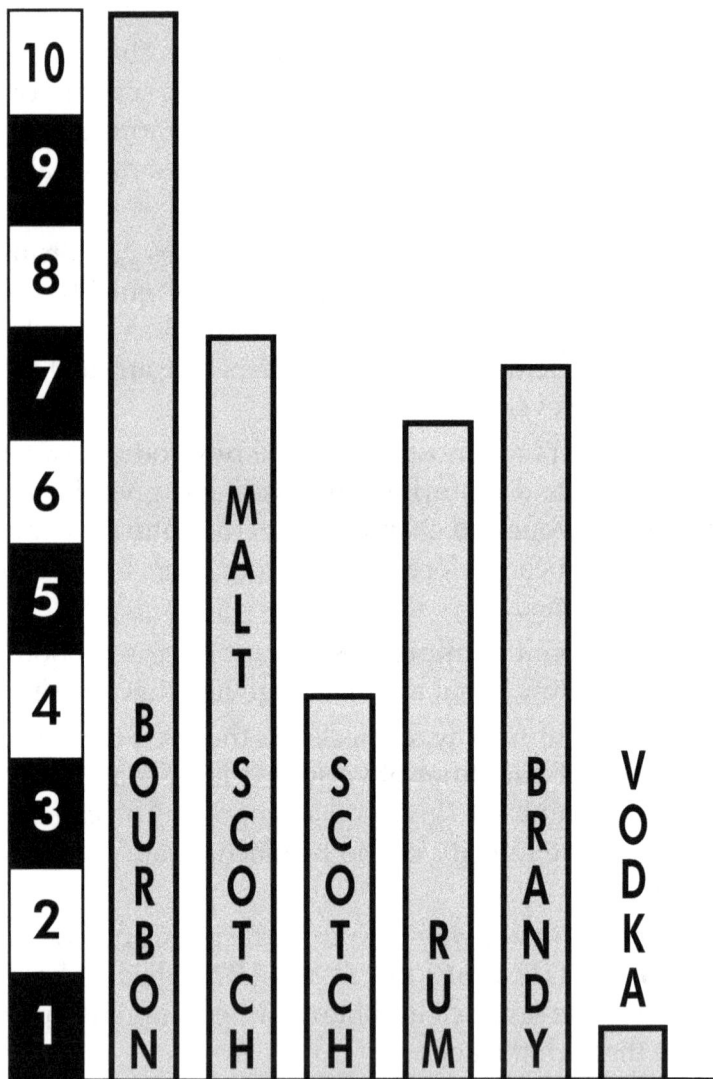

Bar chart showing hangover severity ratings on a scale of 1 to 10: BOURBON 10, MALT SCOTCH 7, SCOTCH 4, RUM 6.5, BRANDY 7, VODKA 1.

MORNING AFTER PAIN

Note: Although beer has the same low amount of impurities as vodka, you need to drink much more beer to get the same kick, so you imbibe many more congeners than if you consumed the same amount of alcohol in vodka.

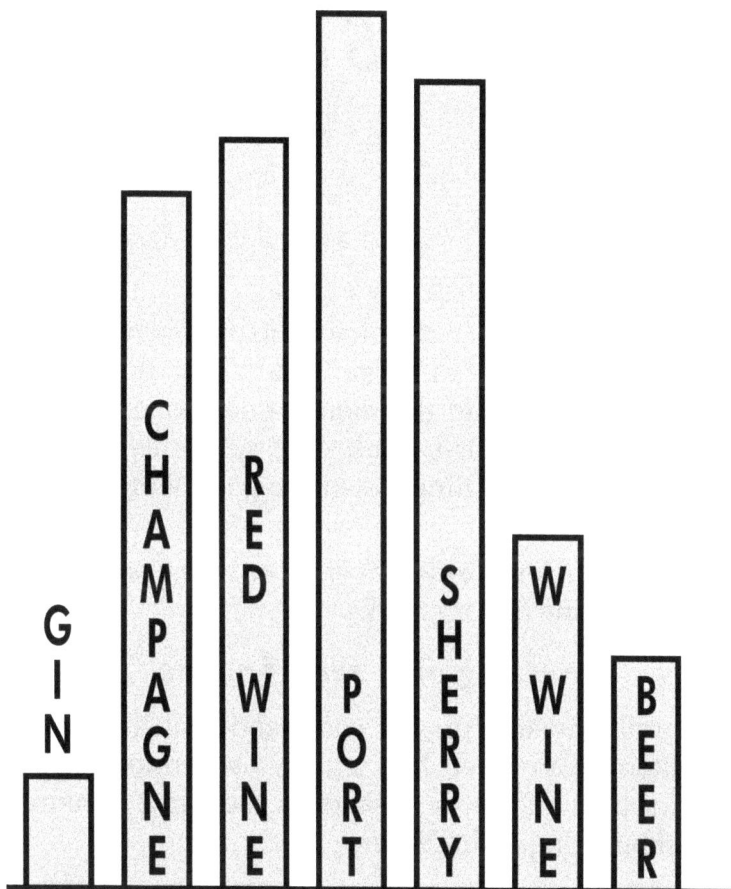

Great drunks of history

No one will ever know who discovered booze, but there can be no doubt that there were drunks from the moment someone sampled that very first drink. And since then personkind has been guzzling down the good stuff in huge quantities.

Here are a few lurid tales of those who drank themselves into the history books.

Sailing on a sea of booze

Admiral Edward Russell, commander of the British Mediterranean Fleet, had a truly stupendous appetite for booze even for a sailor in the hand-drinking, swashbuckling 17th Century.

After trying — and almost succeeding — to drink

dry all of Spain, he threw his booziest party starting on 26 November 1694 at his sumptuous headquarters in the Spanish town of Alicante.

A group of government officials from London were visiting, and to impress them, the red-nosed Admiral turned the entire outdoor fountain in the garden into a huge punch bowl!

It was so big that a row-boat could float around it, manned by a young sailor who served up punch for the thirsty guests. But the fumes were so potent that the sailor had to be replaced every 15 minutes to prevent him passing out.

The party went on for an entire week, with a silk canopy going up when it started to rain to prevent the punch from being diluted.

The Admiral and his guests — more than 6000 attended during the course of the week — drank and drank each day till they passed out, then started again next morning. The party only ended when the row-boat ran aground for lack of punch.

If you reckon you'd like to recreate the good Admiral's hospitality (and your pocket can stand it), here's the recipe for his gigantic punch:

Four hogsheads (1150 litres) of brandy

1135 litres of Malaga wine

90 litres of lime juice

591kg of brown sugar

2500 lemons

2kg of grated nutmeg

500 litres of water.

Cut the lemons into quarters and mix all the ingredients together in one outdoor fountain or small pool, using the oars of a boat to stir until all the ingredients are dissolved. Drink with several thousand friends.

My kingdom (and my wife!) for a bottle

George IV (nicknamed Prinny) was England's most drunken and fattest king ever — and not without reason. Even when suffering from an inflamed bladder, rheumatism and gout, his breakfast would consist of three beefsteaks and two pigeons, washed down with a bottle of wine, half a bottle of champagne, two glasses of port and "several" glasses of brandy.

It is claimed his wife drove Prinny to drink when he was still the Prince of Wales. He first met his foul-smelling bride, Caroline of Brunswick, three days before their wedding and discovered she had not yet adopted the English custom of washing and changing her clothes at least once a week.

Prinny was so revolted by her smell that he hurriedly kissed her, then went to a corner of the room and started drinking brandy — and never completely sobered up again.

Prinny was still in his cups on their wedding day in April 1795, spending the night in a drunken stupor on the floor of the royal bedroom.

So much did Prinny despise his wife that, at their coronation on 19 July 1821, he ordered guards to lock the doors to prevent her getting in. Of course, the good king, who by now weighted more than 17 stone, was again almost blotto, so he had to be supported into Westminster Abbey by eight noblemen.

At the reception that followed, he drank bottle after bottle of brandy. The royal physician was on standby and every time the king passed out he was bled until he revived — only to continue drinking and eating.

Stinking Caroline certainly had enough vices to drive any man to drink. Even before she married her royal cousin, she shocked the crowned heads of Europe by turning up topless at a society ball in Geneva, dipping her nipples into the champagne glasses to cool down.

On another occasion she joined a hunting party wearing only a pumpkin on her head, explaining that "nothing is so cool or so comfortable".

Welsh shall we have another?

Welsh poet Dylan Thomas boasted that he was "the most drunken man in the world" and once travelled to America as part of his "insatiable quest for naked women in wet mackintoshes".

Born on 27 October 1914, he said he was driven to drink by the Tax Collector, who snatched all his earnings before he even received them after he fell behind with his tax payments for a few years.

Whatever the reason, he certainly drank more than he ever paid in taxes.

He particularly loved American and Canadian whiskeys and became so inspiring when drunk that many rich people vied with one another to buy him drinks.

Even at work at the staid BBC, where booze was banned, Thomas managed to keep himself going by

sipping from a bottle marked "champagne wine tonic", ostensibly for his health.

He was on air one morning when he suddenly drained the bottle, stopped talking for a moment, then remarked: "Somebody's boring me — I think it's me!" Then he walked off in search of another drink.

Thomas was only 39 when, one November night in New York, he set out on a final drinking binge — shortly after his doctors had told him to give up drink altogether. Before he collapsed, he said proudly: "I've had 18 straight whiskeys. I think that's a record."

He died in St Vincent's Hospital, New York, where the cause of death was given as "an acute alcoholic insult to the brain".

Another Welshman, Dr Clive Arkle, was so drunk so often that police took away his firearms licence because of his "intemperate habits and lack of competitive activity".

The doctor went to court to prove them wrong. He testified that his regular daily drop of 30 pints of bitter was only enough to "tighten up the eyeballs" — and produced a mass of trophies which he had won after one such visit to the pub. His appeal, strangely enough, was disallowed.

Dr Arkle took an oath on the Bible and then testified with his hands hanging by his sides, so the magistrate was probably suspicious about his testimony.

The reason for this is simple: the English word testimony has a very unusual origin. When ancient Romans, drunk or sober, swore an oath to tell the truth, they solemnly placed their right hand on their testicles and only then were they allowed to testify. Whether about tightening eyeballs or anything else ...

Noah your drinks and you'll live longer

The joy of a booze-up and the agony of a hangover began with Noah, or so the Bible tells us. For, as we read in Genesis, "Noah, the tiller of the soil, was the first (man in the world) to plant a vineyard. And he drank of the wine and became drunk."

Drunk as a skunk, in fact, for he passed out stark naked in his tent! But a good session with the bottle (or was it a leather cask in those days?) certainly did

49

NOAH!! You've only got ONE of each animal!!

CRIPES!! I must have been seeing DOUBLE!

Noah no harm. He not only survived being seasick on the Ark, but lived to the ripe old age of 950!

Here's to you and your ghost!

When Philip the Handsome of Spain died almost 500 years ago, having drunk himself to death, his wife Joanna took to drink — and never again became sober enough to leave their marital bed.

For company, she kept Philip's corpse in bed next to her for three years, drinking toasts to his health every morning and evening. Her subjects named her Joanna the Mad.

The smells from the corpse (no longer handsome) finally forced the servants to remove it after Joanna passed out one day — and she continued toasting it, never even realising it had gone!

In Like Flynn (and Niven) at Cirrhosis-by-the-Sea

Errol Flynn and David Niven shared a house in Hollywood they aptly named "Cirrhosis-by-the-Sea". For a while the two dabbled with other drugs as well, until they settled down and concentrated on booze.

Flynn later admitted he had used everything from mainlining heroin to a pinch of cocaine on his penis — as an aphrodisiac.

When he was drunk — and that was often — the Tasmanian-bom Flynn loved nothing better than a good old bar-room brawl, which he usually won.

The two almost succeeded in drinking Hollywood dry, and in the process established an amazing reputation for wenching and wild behaviour.

As Sheridan Morley recounts in his biography of Niven, *The Other Side of the Moon*, "Flynn and Niven were a couple of the likeliest lads around town. Female stars were extra-

51

maritally bedded, films made, bars were broken up; it was a case of 'no job too big to too small' ... David was able to revert to the teenage tearaway who had smuggled a prostitute into his public school."

Among these drunken exploits was smuggling Joan Bennett into Flynn's bedroom at Cirrhosis-by-the-Sea under the nose of her understandably aggrieved husband Walter Wanger — who later shot another man in the testicles for merely making a pass at Joan!

Lusty Pope's wine, women and song

Early Popes featured prominently among the great drunks of history.

Pope John XII was a prime example. Born in Rome around 837, he was only 18 when he took over the Holy See and introduced one of the most drunken and depraved reigns in Catholic history.

This earned him the nickname "The Christian Caligula".

Pope John threw constant parties at which female pilgrims were not only raped and man-handled, but also sent to work as prostitutes in the Lateran Palace.

His palace guard was a gang of cut-throats who robbed and terrorised the city as they sought new virgins for the Pope to enjoy.

Almost never sober — when he was, he suffered from a terrible hangover — the Pope once ordained a bishop in a stable and took great pleasure from watching priests who had angered him being mutilated.

He died at the age of 27 — very drunk and in the arms of his mistress.

To mix a drink called a **Pope**, you need:

Tokay (a rich, sweet and aromatic Hungarian wine)

Ripe bitter oranges

Sugar, nutmeg and cloves

Pour the wine, hot or cold, over the oranges, mix in sugar and spices to taste.

To mix a **Cardinal**, use red wine such as claret or burgundy, instead of Tokay; for a **Bishop**, substitute white instead of red wine.

Drunk and disorderly! Who, me?

Arthur Mason takes the title as arguably the greatest British drunk of modern times.

After being convicted for the 59th time of being

drunk and disorderly, the magistrate informed the amiable drunk that no publican in his native Basingstoke would ever be allowed to serve him again.

In fact, the court ruled, they would be guilty of an offence if they did.

But Arthur was too drunk to understand — so the magistrate had to wait until the next day when he had sobered up to inform him of the ban.

When the sentence finally sank in, Arthur found a way to outwit the law — he moved to the next town!

French General Bisson, one of Napoleon's right-hand men during his ill-fated invasion of Russia, drank eight bottles of wine every day — with breakfast!

The sweetest way to die?

Grieved by the death of his favourite brother-in-law, the drunken old Anglo-Saxon King Hundung decided to drown his sorrows — literally!

He called all his noblemen together for a feast and had a huge vat of mead (wine made from honey) placed in the centre of the hall. When his guests had drunk their fill and were about to pass out, the good king threw himself into the vat and drowned.

Another drunken king also used wine to kill — but this time the victim was not himself. England's King Edward IV forced his brother George, Duke of Clarence, to drink himself to death — literally.

He had George put to death in the Tower of London in 1478 by drowning him in a tub of sweet Malmsey wine, because he felt threatened by George's sober habits.

Other famous people also died strangely.

Aeschylus, father of Greek drama, was killed in 456 BC by a tortoise dropped on his bald head by an eagle! The bird, keen to break the shell, had apparently mistaken the shiny dome for a stone.

Experimenting with refrigeration (to make ice for his drinks?), the philosopher Francis Bacon was stuffing a chicken with snow in 1626 when he caught a cold — that killed him.

Song of the Vodka Boatmen

Is the Russian town of Krasnensk, in Byelorussia, home to the biggest boozers in the world? Judge for yourself.

The town has a population of only 6000, yet consumes 150,000 bottles of vodka a month — an average of 25 bottles per person, including children!

'I bet you don't know this ... '

How would you like to stand in the pub all night and win round after round of free drinks? Then you're in luck. By reading *The Hangover Handbook*, you are about to make that dream come true — while you amuse your mates at the same time.

The following 20 questions should each be worth a round of drinks — unless of course someone else in the bar has been wise enough also to buy a copy of *The Hangover Handbook*!

All the answers appear in the book, but in case you want to quiz your mates before you've read it all, you'll find out where to look by turning to the last page.

1. Name the famous poet who called himself "the most drunken man in the world" and lusted after "naked women in wet mackintoshes"?
2. How do you say "hangover" in German?
3. How do voodoo priests cure hangovers?

4. Which two famous drinkers named their home Cirrhosis-by-the-Sea?

5. What is a teetotaller?

6. Which idiots first taxed booze?

7. How do you say "Cheers" in Welsh?

8. What are the impurities called that scientists blame for hangovers?

9. How did lusty King Henry VIII punish palace staff who made female servants pregnant?

10. What distance does alcohol travel through your bloodstream before your entire body is pickled?

11. Which famous boozer said: "A woman drove me to drink — and I never even wrote to thank her"?

12. Where is wine called "the milk of the elderly"?

13. How do you make Scots Guts and Highland Honey?

14. Why is St Brigid of Ireland loved by drinkers and disliked by brewers?

15. Who advocated the following hangover cure: "A barrel of oysters, a dish of neats' tongues, a dish of anchovies, wine of all sorts and Northdowne Ale"?

16. Why did the wines of ancient Egypt and ancient Libya keep drinkers running to the loo?

17. How do you mix an alcoholic Pope, an alcoholic Cardinal and an alcoholic Bishop outside the Catholic Church?

18. Which country boasts the largest beer consumption in the world?

19. Who was Mr Grog?

20. Which right royal tippler believed that the only hangover cure was warm brandy liberally spiced with pepper?

(Answers on Page 162)

The pub talk survivor's guide

Mixing drinks does not make you drunk — it's the amount of alcohol in each drink that's the culprit. But starting the night with beer and then switching to spirits can make you drunk more quickly than you'd imagine.

The reason is simple: your palate gets dulled by the beer and can't appreciate the strength of the spirits. So you toss them down at the same rate as the beer, consuming a lot more alcohol than you think you are. Don't say you haven't been warned!

Coffee? No thanks!

Strong coffee is no antidote for booze — but can actually make matters worse, according to a Sydney University research team.

They found that caffeine produced "a wide-awake

drunk who could be more dangerous because if he had not taken the coffee he would have been more aware of the impairment of his other faculties".

Get tanked up in style

The world's largest pewter beer tankard, made in Malaysia in 1985, can hold 2796 litres, enough to give several hundred people a giant hangover!

What a way for a drink to go!

The human body has 206 bones and 96,000 kilometres of blood vessels, some so thin that blood corpuscles can only pass through in single file. Impurities in booze chasing through those thin veins cause the throbbing ache and sick feeling we call a hangover.

What to do when the dog bites

Why do people refer to the morning-after drink that cures a hangover as "a hair of the dog that bit you"?

In the days when superstition and medical science were one, it was believed that the bite from a mad dog could be cured by putting some of its hairs on the wound. The first reference to the term in English occurred in 1546.

Brown champagne by royal command

Frederick the Great of Prussia loved drinking coffee — if it was made with champagne. It is not known what cure he used for champagne-coffee hangovers.

At this clinic, the cure ends with a cuppa!

The world's first hangover clinic opened in London in 1971 and offered sufferers the following treatment:

First, you have a sauna to sweat out the last of the alcohol still lurking in your bloodstream. This is followed by a fruit-sugar preparation laced with vitamins B1, B6, C and garden mint. Next you are given a few gulps of pure oxygen.

Then, to help your screaming intestines absorb all that goodness, you get a "gentle and sympathetic massage", a spirit alcohol rub and, as a grand finale and tribute to the virtues of teetotalism, a nice strong cuppa tea.

Boasted Managing Director Connor Walsh: "You go out fresh as a two-year-old!"

Why love is like a cocktail party

The energy expended by humans in a single act of lovemaking is the same as that needed to stand at cocktail parties and make small talk for about eight hours.

And while on the subject of mating games: Cobras take between two minutes and 24 hours to mate, while snails can keep at it for up to 12 hours. Impala often make love on the run.

How Randy King Henry saved beer money

King Henry VIII, whose lust for female flesh led to the founding of the Church of England, insisted that his male staff should be punished if they indulged in extra-marital sex.

The regulations for his Officers of the Bedchamber stated: "Such pages as cause the maids of the King's household to become mothers will go without beer for a month."

Nelson's blood!

After the battle of Waterloo, Admiral Lord Nelson was shipped back to England in a cask of brandy, so that his body would be fresh for the State funeral. When the corpse was removed, the brandy was given to sailors so they could drink a toast to their departed commander — which they happily did.

Miracle of the bathtub

Perhaps the most welcome miracle performed by a Catholic Saint was when St Brigid of Ireland changed her bath water into beer for thirsty visitors to her

Kildare abbey in the 1500s.

The refreshed band of drinkers reported afterwards that the beer had a "saintlike" quality and taste.

And while on the subject of bizarre stories about saints: Pontius Pilate has been canonised as a Saint in the Ethiopian Church.

Blasted booze!

Most people who indulge in a tipple know that spirits are a certain percentage proof, which indicates the relative quantities of water and alcohol in the mixture.

Scientifically, proof spirit has a specific gravity of 12 over 13 at 51 degrees F.

The original proof test employed a more practical kind of science: spirit poured over gunpowder and lit would eventually fire the powder if it was proof; if under-proof, the water remaining after the alcohol had burned off would prevent the powder from igniting.

Heidi's brew packs a punch

The world's most potent beer is brewed in Switzerland. Samichlaus Bier has 13.7 per cent alcohol.

That's only part of the story ...

The Czech Republic boasts the largest beer consumption in the world — 148.6 litres a year for every man, woman and child. Which means some men must drink a lot more than that! Australia ranks eleventh, with 83.1 litres downed per person each year.

No room for beer bellies

Australia's smallest pub can be seen in the heart of Kalgoorlie, where it did brisk business between 1899 and 1924. A mere 3.35 metres wide, the British Arms was strategically placed opposite the busy Hannan Street station, which meant it quenched the thirst of miners both coming to and leaving the fabulously rich Western Australian goldfield. Today it is the Gold Mile Museum, which boasts many fascinating goldrush relics.

To drink, or not to drink ...

In Manitoba, Canada, local law prohibits you drinking beer in the loo. And in the Canadian province of Saskatchewan, it is illegal to drink water in a beer parlour.

Was that you I saw drinking beer out of an old shoe?!

Yeah, but it was Laced!!

Give love the boozer's boot

Egyptians believed you could cure love-sickness by drinking beer out of an old shoe.

Monk(ey) business in Olde England

John, King of England from 1199 to 1216, liked a new kind of beer prepared in his honour so much that he drank himself to death with it!

Then, in an attempt to convince St Peter their king was not a drunk but a holy man, his loyal subjects dressed him in a monk's outfit for his burial.

Plastered on a penny!

The phrase beer money goes back around 200 years. English soldiers traditionally received a ration of beer every day, the equivalent of the naval nip of rum or grog (watered down rum). Between 1800 and 1823 they were given an allowance of a penny a day beer money instead, which eventually became synonymous with money to be spent on pleasure.

Dutch courage

A former Dutch military custom of drinking spirits, particularly gin, before going into battle is the most likely origin of the derogatory idiom *Dutch courage*.

What bad word starts with a T?

That horrible word teetotal was invented by a New York temperance society which demanded that new members put a huge "T" next to their names whenever they signed them to signify Total abstinence from booze. They soon became known as T-totals and gave the English language the word teetotal.

The five reasons for drinking

Good wine, a friend, or being dry,
Or lest we should be by and by,
or any other reason why ...

The taxman always taketh

The first known tax on booze was introduced in 3400 BC in the Ancient Egyptian city of Memphis, on the Nile. The tax was charged on barley wine. Strange as it sounds, it was actually the first known form of beer.

Grog has a human face

When you go on the grog, you're actually drinking to the memory of Admiral Edward Vernon, who got the nickname "Old Grog" because he wore a cloak of coarse cloth called grogram.

The admiral was labelled a cheapskate when in 1740 he ordered that Royal Navy sailors could no longer have their neat half-pint of rum, but that it should be diluted with water. This mixture immediately became known as grog.

With his sailors no longer pie-eyed by noon, Old Grog actually won some naval battles. So the Navy decided grog was a good thing — and henceforth it was the only drink issued to sailors.

The daily grog ration was only abolished in 1970.

Mother's milk!

The weekly children's food ration in a British hospital in 1632 included two gallons of beer.

First drops Down Under

Australia's first brewery was started by John Boston, who used maize and the leaves and stalks of the Cape gooseberry to brew beer in 1796 in Sydney. The first government brewery was opened in Parramatta in 1804.

HolyXXX!

In the Middle Ages, beer did not include hops and was not preserved, so you drank it as you made it — and that kept the monks who were the main brewers in Merrie Olde England very merry indeed!

It was the monks who first put crosses — later to become the signs "XX" and "XXX" — on beer barrels to indicate that the beer inside had been brewed in the monastery and was of guaranteed quality.

What a weird Libyan libation

The Libyans, 2400 years ago, had a weird way to prevent hangovers after their mammoth wine drinking orgies: they mixed their wine with sea water! This made them so sick they never got really drunk enough to suffer. The historian Strabo says they spent much of the feast time in the loo.

These fellahs know their booze

What is booze? Strictly speaking, it's a potent beer-like brew made from barley by the good fellahs of Egypt.

To make *Boozah*, as they call it, they place barley in an earthenware vessel which is buried in the ground. When the barley starts to germinate, it is crushed, made into a dough and baked until a crust forms. The crust is dried and carried around the desert with the fellahs in the form of a cake.

When they reach an oasis, instead of drinking the water, they use it to dissolve this cake of dehydrated beer, which immediately starts to ferment.

Within hours they'd have enough boozah to make them very merry — and provide a "hair of the dog" in the morning.

Western travellers who sampled the brew wrote about it in English and the name was soon applied to all kinds of alcoholic drinks — and to the boozers who enjoy them.

Egyptian wines, reported the Roman historian Pliny around the time of Christ, were "remarkable for their sweetness and laxative qualities".

He wrote: "Wines which are more carefully mixed with sea water do not cause headache. They loosen the bowels, excite the stomach, cause inflation and assist digestion."

In France, wine is affectionately known as "the milk of the elderly".

Steamy tale of beer and brewers

The first steam engine used in a brewery is still in existence and can be seen at the Powerhouse Museum in Sydney.

Built by Boulton and Watt of Birmingham, the steam engine was first used in the Whitbread brewery in England in 1785 and shipped to Australia 102 years later.

Thirsty Sandgropers

Australia's only hangover study, carried out a few years ago, showed Western Australia leading the field, with 38 per cent of those polled suffering at least one hangover during the short survey period.

New South Wales came second with 28 per cent, followed by South Australia, Victoria, Tasmania and Queensland.

... And thirstier Scots

In 1842 the Scots — men, women and children together — drank a staggering 5,595,186 gallons of whisky, equal to more than two gallons each.

American whiskey is called Bourbon because it was first made in Bourbon County, Kentucky, in 1789.

St Patrick not only chased all the snakes from Ireland, but tradition has it that he also introduced the then barbaric Irish tribes to the fine art of distilling Irish whisky.

Apparently the holy man liked a tipple or two himself!

Do you smell a rat?

The custom of embracing women by their friends and relatives was introduced, reports Joseph Haydn in his *Dictionary of Dates*, "by the early Romans not out of respect, but to found out by their breath whether they had been drinking wine, this being criminal for women to do, as it sometimes led to adultery".

Pie-eyed for love!

Having a sweetheart with a long name could easily

turn you into a drunk in Roman times. When toasting her, tradition demanded that you drink a cup of wine for every letter in her name.

Grime and grease pack a punch

Pollution is not all bad — it makes for strong beer and ale. At least that was the belief of the Brewers' Guide of London in 1702, when it provided this recipe for making extra potent ale:

"Thames water taken up about Greenwich at Low-water when it is free from all brackishness of the sea and it has all the Fat and Sullage of this great city of London, makes very strong drink.

"It will all itself ferment wonderfully and after its due purgations and three times stinking, it will be so strong that several Sea commanders have told me that it has often fuddled their murriners."

Roman way to lead a damsel astray

Vermouth has not always been only a vital ingredient in cocktails — in Roman times the forerunner of today's vermouth was hailed as a powerful aphrodisiac.

One Roman guide for young blades advised: "Take elecampane, the seeds of flowers, vervain and berries of mistletoe.

"Dry them well in the oven, then beat them into a powder and give it to the party you design upon in a glass of wine and it will work wonderful effect to your advantage."

TOMBSTONE TRIBUTES

✝

Here John Randal lies
Who counting of his tale
Lived threescore years and ten,
Such vertue was in ale.
Ale was his meat,
Ale was his drink,
Ale did his heart revive,
And if he could have drunk his ale
He still had been alive.
He died January 5,
1699.

✝

Ob. 1741
Rebecca Freeland,
She drank good ale, good punch and wine,
And lived to the age of 99.

In vino, veritas

They say many a true word is spoken in jest — and the same applies to wine. The old Romans knew that only too well, as their famous proverb testifies: *In vino, veritas* (In wine, the truth). In this chapter, some of the greatest wits and wisest men ever to take a drink, share the true spirit of the vine with us.

Oh God, that men should put an enemy in their mouths to steal away their brains.

—SHAKESPEARE.

The only way to get rid of temptation is to yield to it.

— OSCAR WILDE.

A woman drove me to drink — and I never even wrote to thank her.

— W.C. FIELDS.

EVERYBODY loves SOMEBODY...

DEAN MARTINI

Dean Martin on how to avoid a hangover: "Stay drunk!"

Author Kingsley Amis has this advice on how to cope with hangovers: "Immediately on waking, start telling yourself how lucky you are to be feeling so bloody awful. This, known as George Gale's paradox, recognises the truth that if you do not feel bloody awful after a hefty night then you are still drunk, and must sober up in a waking state before the hangover dawns!"

"Water, taken in moderation, never hurt anybody," said Mark Twain. But before you decide to drink only water, consider the following facts. To fill a Texas "ten-gallon" hat you need only three-quarters of a gallon of water. A jellyfish consists 95.4 per cent of water, while the water content of an adult human is between 58 and 66 per cent of body weight.

> *And Noah he often said to his wife*
> *when he sat down to dine,*
> *'I don't care where the water goes*
> *if it doesn't get into the wine.'*
>
> — GILBERT KEITH CHESTERTON.

In the order named these are the hardest to control: wine, women and song!

> — FRANKLIN P. ADAMS.

> God made the Vine,
> Was it a sin
> That Man made Wine
> To drown trouble in?
>
> — OLIVER HERFORD.

> *Wine is the drink of the gods,*
> *milk the drink of babies,*
> *tea the drink of women,*
> *and water the drink of beasts.*
>
> — JOHN STUART BLACKIE.

Dean Martin, a great fan on the odd drop: "I feel sorry for people who don't drink. When they wake up in the morning that's as good as they are going to feel all day long."

> *A meal without wine is a day without sunshine.*
>
> — LOUIS VAUDABLE, owner of Maxim's, Paris.

If with water you fill up your glasses,
You'll never write anything wise;
For wine is the horse of Parnassus,
Which hurries a bard to the skies.

— THOMAS MOORE.

A teetotaller is the very worst sort of drunkard.

— E.F. BENSON.

*There was once a man who learnt to mind
his own business. He went to heaven.
I hope teetotallers will remember that.*

— T.W.H. CROSLAND.

**I'm only a beer teetotaller,
not a champagne teetotaller.**

— GEORGE BERNARD SHAW.

I do not drink more than a sponge.

— French author FRANCOIS RABELAIS.

A good Martini should be strong enough
to make your eyeballs bubble,
and so cold your teeth will ache,
and you'll think you're hearing sleigh bells.

— L.G. SHREVE.

**There are two things that will be believed
of any man whatsoever,
and one of them is that
he has taken to drink.**

— BOOTH TARKINGTON.

Scotch whisky to a Scotchman is as innocent as
milk is to the rest of the human race.

— MARK TWAIN.

While beer brings gladness, don't forget
That water only makes you wet.

— HARRY LEON WILSON.

Here's to good old Whiskey
So amber and clear.
'Tis not so sweet as woman's lips
But a damned sight more sincere.

— LEWIS C. HENRY.

The rapturous, wide and ineffable pleasure
of drinking at someone else's expense.

— HENRY S. LEIGH.

I reminded him of that old saying,
'There are more old drunkards
than old doctors.'

— J.P. MCEVOY.

I drink only to make my friends seem interesting.

— DON MARQUIS.

There is nothing wrong with sobriety in moderation.

— JOHN CIARDI.

'Twas honest old Noah first planted the Vine
And mended his Morals by drinking its Wine ...

— BENJAMIN FRANKLIN.

One drink is just right,
two are too many,
three are too few.

— SPANISH SAYING.

One swallow does not make a summer
but too many swallows make a fall.

— GEORGE PRENTICE.

There are two reasons for drinking:
one is when you are thirsty, to cure it;
the other, when you are not thirsty,
to prevent it.

— THOMAS LOVE PEACOCK.

Men with short necks got no business drinking
neat whiskey. It don't have time to cool. It hits
their stomachs red hot and burns 'em right out.

— WALLACE MORTON.

Why has the good old custom of coming
together to get drunk gone out?
Think of the delight of drinking
in pleasant company and then
lying down to sleep a deep long sleep.

— NATHANIEL HAWTHORNE.

Author G.E.W. Russell described whiskey as "A torchlight
procession marching down your throat".

"Scotch whisky is made from barley and the
morning dew on angel's nipples."

— WARREN ELLIS.

77

A hangover by any other name

Hangovers are a universal phenomenon. Chances are that one fine day you're going to wake up in a strange country with the usual symptoms.

To ensure they don't cart you off to the morgue there and then, your first priority will be to explain your condition so you can get help fast!

Here's what you say:

Spain: *Resaca* (means "ailment")

Italy: *Malessere dopo una sbornia* ("Ailment after drink")

Germany: *Katzenjammer* ("Wailing of cats")

France: *Gueule de bois* ("wooden throat")

Sweden: *Hont i haret* ("A pain in the roots of the hair")

Denmark: *Tommermaend* ("Carpenters")

Norway: *Jeg har tommermen* ("Carpenters in my head")

Netherlands: *Kater* ("Cat")

Poland: *Kociokwik* ("Wailing of kittens").

Beer, glorious beer!

BEER makes you feel as you ought to feel without beer, observed the famous poet and beer lover Henry Lawson. Shakespeare called it "a dish fit for a king".

Today billions around the world agree with heady delight, quaffing their way through many thousands of different brands of this golden brew of the gods.

Small "boutique" breweries, some only catering for one pub, are springing up everywhere — and thriving. Imported beer sales are booming, even though they often cost two or three times the price of standard, mass-produced local brews. Beer lists are increasingly becoming available at restaurants. Home brewing by enthusiasts wanting quality rather than just low cost is increasing dramatically. The world, without doubt, is in the midst of a beer revolution.

Origins

Where did beer and ale originate? In 1922, scientists working in Iran discovered a jar at Goden Tepe which was carbon dated as coming from late 4000 BC.

The grooves of the jar were found to contain a substance known as calcium oxalate. This is the main component of "beerstone", a deposit left by drinks brewed from barley. Although these oxalates could have come from other products, such as rhubarb, it is considered most unlikely that the jar would have been used to store anything other than liquid — in other words, a fermented barley drink.

The brewers of this drink were Sumerians, one of the oldest literate civilisations. They employed a relatively complicated system of agriculture utilising irrigation to grow cereal crops, including barley.

To convert the starch found in barley into a soluble form, the Sumerians probably made bread! A sourdough would have been added to the fresh barley and the resultant mixture made into loaves. These loaves, when broken up and added to water, would have fermented easily.

The ancient Egyptians praised the gods for everything — including the creation of beer, although sadly it appears the amber nectar was born in blood.

The oldest recorded example of brewing, found in Egyptian hieroglyphics carved in stone during the reign of King Seti I, tell how the goddess Hathor came to earth one night in such a fury that she slaughtered everyone in her way.

The streets were literally running with blood, so Ra,

the Sun god, ordered fruit to be mixed with ground barley and the running blood. That night Ra used the mixture to cover the fields where Hathor had been in bloody action.

When she returned at dawn, she saw her face reflected in the mixture. So enchanted was she with her looks that she bent down and drank the beer until she became so sozzled she forgot all about further killing.

After that, wise priestesses averted further slaughter by regularly offering beer as a sacrifice at Hathor's altars.

When Egyptian pharaoh Rameses III died around 1200 B.C., his greatest achievements during his life were inscribed on his tomb. They included the fact

that he had offered exactly 446,303 jugs of beer to the gods. Unfortunately, there is no record of how many jugs the pious king consumed himself.

Beer Down Under

To cater for the thirsts of 95 men on board the *Endeavour*, Captain Cook laid in 1200 gallons of beer when he set off on his exploration of the Pacific — and within a month of sailing all but two casks had been drunk.

It was Cook's thirsty sailors who brewed the first beer in New Zealand, at Dusky Sound in 1772. Officially it was to combat scurvy, but one would assume that the Jack Tars also imbibed for the sheer pleasure of it.

The first brewery on the Land of the Long White Cloud was set up in 1831 by Joel Samuel Polack at Kororareka.

Australia's first ale was brewed by John Boston, a free settler who arrived in New South Wales in October 1794, using maize and leaves and stalks of the Cape gooseberry for his popular concoction.

In an attempt to reduce the huge consumption of rum, the British government almost a decade later agreed to a suggestion from Governor King and shipped out "six bags of hops, and two complete sets of brewing materials".

Using these, commercial brewing in Australia started when the country's first — and only — government brewery was set up in Parramatta in September 1804 by Thomas Rushdon.

To keep supplies flowing, the authorities agreed that anyone who owned the government money could pay not only in coin but also in barley, with a Governor's Order of 1 October 1804 stating: "The raising and supplying of barley will greatly depend on the settlers, in exchange for which they are assured beer."

As supplies of barley poured in, the brewery within six months of opening stepped up production from 1800 gallons a week to 6888 gallons for sale — after paying many of its bills for work and materials in liquid gold.

Soon, however, Government employees started drinking the brewery dry, each being allowed five gallons free a week, so after a year Governor King reported the brewery had been running a loss and arranged to sell it, with brewmaster Rushdon being the successful tenderer.

He sold "table beer" at sixpence a gallon and "strong beer" at a shilling a gallon.

A few months after the Parramatta brewery was established, it encountered opposition from a rival set up by Mr P. L. Larken in Castlereagh Street, Sydney, who published the following advertisement in the *Sydney Gazette* on 23 December 1804:

LARKEN'S BREWERY. Ales — Pale, Brown and Amber; Twopenny, and London Porter, etc., prepared after the system of the British breweries. The advertiser respectfully hopes that the general introduction of these wholesome, long and justly celebrated English beverages, as well as tending to supersede the too destructive use of ardent spirits, will recommend the present undertaking to the attention of the colony from its prompt conduciveness to health, sobriety, and economy.

By 1814, four breweries were operating in Sydney alone. One of these brewers, Daniel Cooper, advertised that his "strong, sound and most wholesome beverage" could be paid for in many unusual ways (including your own house, if your thirst was really great!):

Payment will be taken in the form of Colonial property; and produce at the market price of the day, whether consisting of land, houses, grain, cattle, sheep, horses, pigs, pork, poultry, eggs, cheese, butter, lard, tallow, wool, hides, leather, shoes, soap, candles, tobacco, hemp, flax, wattle-bark, salt, kangaroo skins, seal skins, fish oil, sawn timber, cedar logs, shingles, lathes, wood fuel or oil. But in case the said produce be not brought to the brewery at the time the beer is purchased payment will be required in Spanish dollars at 5/- each.

Australia's best known international brand, Foster's Lager, was first brewed by two brothers named (you guessed it!} Foster in 1888 in Melbourne.

They were the only brewers in the town to boast an ice-making machine, which not only enabled them to make lager beer, but also to supply pubs with ice so they could serve Foster's Lager ice cold.

From this is said to have developed the Australian tradition of drinking very cold beer.

A closer look

So what is this amazing liquid we call beer and what about such close relatives as ale and stout?

Why are some beers light-coloured and others dark, some mind-blowingly potent and some extra mild, some old and others new?

And how do master brewers create such an amazing range of tastes using four classic ingredients: barley, hops, yeast and water?

Beer is made from the brewing and fermentation of cereals, usually malted barley, and flavoured with hops to give it a bitter taste. Fungus yeast converts the sugars in the malted barley to alcohol, but if the alcohol content gets too high it kills the yeast, making it impossible to brew very strong beer.

Barley malt brewing produces three fundamental products — beer, ale and lager. Originally in England, ale and beer meant the same thing, until around the 14th century when hops was introduced and beer came to mean hopped ale.

Traditional beer and ale is top fermented (that is, the yeast floats on the top), while lager (the most popular beer in Australia and the most widely drunk beer in the world today) is bottom fermented.

Lager — which means "storage" — was first brewed in a Bavarian monastery in the 14th century. Because it needs a low fermentation temperature, until the invention of refrigeration lagers were brewed next to lakes that froze over in winter.

Lagers are light coloured, have a medium hop flavour, dry taste, high carbonation and an alcohol content usually between 3 and 4 per cent.

Internationally, the most famous lagers include Dortmund, Munich and California Steam Beer.

Top fermented beers, which are particularly popular in Britain, include ale, stout and porter.

Ale was the first drink produced in Australia, way back in 1794 by John Boston; today, the best known and most popular is Cooper's Sparkling Ale from South Australia.

Stout was originally brewed — and called "stoutt" — as a thick and very potent drink which was served like a liqueur in small fluted glasses. Women loved this drink, because it was supposed to keep their shape in the way men then thought attractive — the kind of buxom stoutness which artists like Rubens and Rembrandt painted with such delight.

The drink was gradually thinned down into the stout we know today, perhaps to keep up with female fashion for a thinner form. Stout gets its dark colour from roasted barley or malt which is included with the normal malt and other ingredients before mashing.

Think of stout and most people today think of Guinness, Ireland's most famous export which, it is claimed, gets its soft and special taste from certain springs in the County Kildare, before being allowed

to mature for a year in oaken vats.

Ale and stout have a stronger, more hoppy flavour than lager and their alcohol content usually ranges between 4-6.5 per cent.

In Germany, since 1615, only barley, hops, yeast and water have been used for brewing hundreds of different varieties of beer, following the promulgation of the Pure Beer Law by Count William IV of Bavaria.

Not so in Australia. A New South Wales Act of 1850 aimed to curb some of the worst concoctions which were being sold as beer.

A brewer faced the then substantial fine of 200 pounds and confiscation of his stock if he should add to his brew "any vitriol coculus indicus nux vomica tobacco opium aloes copperas faba amara or any extract or preparation thereof..."

And if you're wondering about "nux vomica" ... it's another term for strychnine!

Today, Australian law stipulates only that certain preservatives such as sulphur dioxide (known as "preservative 220") be declared when the product contains more than 25 milligrains per kilograin.

Otherwise there is no requirement for brewers (or the makers of any other alcoholic beverage) to declare what ingredients go into them.

Lots of beer contains colourings and flavourings, hop extracts, enzymes and preservatives.

In fact, some of the additives used in the past were apparently quite detrimental to the health of heavy drinkers, such as cobalt salts used in the 1960s (but now abandoned) to improve beer's foaming qualities.

Additives now allowed for beer are: propylene glycol alginate, sulphur dioxide, ascorbic acid or erythorbic acid, caramel, tannic acid, papain, bromelain and ficin.

Today, more than 1500 different beers are brewed commercially in Australia, New Zealand, Britain and North America, ranging from the blackest stout to the palest of pale ales.

And there is a big trend towards "pure beer", which relies on traditional ingredients and the brewmaster, rather than additives, to achieve great taste.

Beer, sex and civilisation

Want to drink a lot of beer and still be in the mood for love? Then a French brewery may have some good news for you real soon.

A heady announcement said the brewery had started tests on a beer, said to contain natural aphrodisiacs, that does not affect the drinker's ability for making love. The beer, it continued, was being tested under strict medical control by 400 drinkers.

Explained Technical Director Marc Arbogast: "It is not a product for Don Juan or marathon love makers, but is meant for men who have experienced sexual inhibitions."

Amazingly, the beer is not very potent (as you would expect for it to release all those inhibitions), but is a mild barley brew with only about 2.5 per cent alcohol, about the same as a typical low-alcohol lager.

"Alcohol is known for its effect of sapping virility and this should reverse the effects," the director added.

So where can you buy this amazing brew? Nowhere yet — and the fact that the news story was published on April Fool's Day should give you some idea of when it is likely to be available. The brewery, of course, denied strenuously that it was playing a practical joke on beer-loving lovers.

And while on the subject of sex, a few years ago *Pageant* magazine, under the headline "Distinguished Doctors Name the Eight Foods That Spark Sexual Desire", reported:

"Peculiarly, of the commonly available foods, beer is the most likely to give women a boost in basic femininity ... The hop is one of the few foods actually containing estrogens ... "

Have a beer? How civilised!

Every beer lover knows the golden brew is the most civilised drink on earth — and now there's anthropological proof for this obvious fact.

It was the discovery of home brewing, about 10,000 years ago, that led our ancestors to settle down and start cultivating crops, according to Dr Solomon Katz of the University of Pennsylvania's Anthropology Department.

He said the event that "primed the pump" of civilisation was the accidental discovery by prehistoric humans that wild wheat and barley, soaked in water to make gruel, if left in the open air did not spoil.

Instead, natural yeast in the air converted it to a

dark, bubbling brew that make whoever drank it feel good. On top of that, the brew made people robust: at the time, it was second only to animal protein as a nutritional source.

Dr Katz said this combination of mood-altering and nutritional properties would have been incentive enough to cause neolithic hunter-gatherers in the Near East to begin cultivating the grains.

He pointed out that the oldest known recipe for brewing beer was found on a Sumerian clay tablet produced over 7000 years ago.

Beware of water!

Medical advice in the time of Shakespeare instructed Englishmen not to drink water because, warned Dr Andrew Boorde in 1542, it was "bad for Englysche men, colde, slow, slacke of digestion".

On the other hand, he noted approvingly, "Ale for an Englysche man is a natural! drinke ... Ale must have these propertyes: It must be fresh and cleare, it must not be ropy or smoky, nor it must be weft or tayle. Ale should not be drinke under V days olde. Newe ale is unwholesome for all men. And sowre (sour) ale, and dead ale the which doth stand a tayle, is good for no man. Barley malte maketh better ale than oaten malte or any other come doth: it doth engendre grose humoures, but yet it maketh a man stronge."

Beer belly blues ...

Why do fervent beer drinkers so often develop beer bellies? It's all the fault of beer's great relaxing qualities, caused by valerianic acid (a relation of Valium).

It relaxes your muscles, particularly in the stomach — and if you drink too much of the good stuff, your belly muscles remain permanently relaxed.

Other factors also help create a beer belly. Warns Dr Kathleen M. Zelman: "A typical beer has 150 calories – and if you down several in one sitting, you can end up with serious calorie overload.

"And don't forget calories from the foods you wash down with those beers. Alcohol can increase your appetite.

"Further, when you're drinking beer at a bar or party, the food on hand is often fattening fare like pizza, wings, and other fried foods."

Horny drinkers made a tumbler

A tumbler today is associated with drinking water rather than beer, yet it's name is directly related to the golden brew.

In Anglo-Saxon days drinking horns were used by beer-loving warriors — and tradition demanded the ale or beer had to be drained in one gulp.

To stop anyone cheating, the horns had rounded bottoms so that when you put one down it would tumble and spill any ale left inside for all to see.

The first glass glasses followed this round-bottomed pattern — and so became known as "tumblers" — and the name stuck even when they acquired flat bottoms.

Gulp, gulp, gulp ... splash ... !

Today the closest we have to a drinking horn is the ale-yard — a trumpet-shaped glass vessel, exactly a yard in length, with a closed narrow end that is expanded into a large ball.

It holds little more than a pint, and when filled with ale or beer the challenge is to empty the entire yard without taking it away your mouth.

This is far from easy, for so long as the tube contains beer, it flows out smoothly, but when air reaches the bulb it displaces the beer with a splash, startling the drinker so that he involuntarily withdraws his mouth. The result? Cold beer all over his face and clothes!

Puzzle out this holy fug

If you thought a yard was hard going, try sampling a Wager or Puzzle fug. In the 17th century these strange beer mugs were great favourites at country inns.

They usually had many spouts, from most of which it was difficult to drink — owing to holes in the neck.

Those in the know used to slurp up the liquor through a secret passage in the hollow handle or through one spout or nozzle — if the drinker had enough fingers to stop up the other spouts and holes during the operation!

On many of these jugs were challenging inscriptions, like this one:

From Mother Earth I claim my birth,
I'm made a joke to man,
But now I'm here, fill'd with good beer
Come, taste me if you can.

Is drinking beer a mug's game?

Germans have a huge range of beer steins, the biggest of which holds four litres. The closest most other countries can come to that is the ordinary beer mug. But have you ever wondered why we call it a "mug"?

If you've ever seen a Toby jug, you'll guess the answer. Actually, the term started in 18th century England where patrons brought their own mugs to alehouses — which soon became known as mughouses — and left them there.

Each mug was uniquely identified with its owner, so anyone's face (his or her unique feature) became their "mug".

And on the subject of beer mugs, why do German steins have lids on them?

Today it is mainly for decoration, but they were introduced by law in the late 16th century to keep insects from falling into the brew and possibly spreading disease.

The law has long since been repealed, but the tradition lives on.

So rough was a pub called The Bells on the Hobart waterfront in Tasmania a century or so ago that the publican served beer in pewter mugs with glass bottoms so a beer drinker could see a fist coming his way while he was taking a swallow!

Ignorance is a lot like alcohol: the more you have of it, the less you are able to see its effect on you.

— JAY M. BYLSMA

The gentle art of pouring

A good beer — and that surely includes your favourite drop — deserves to be served at the right temperature and in a way that best brings out its full flavour.

So, unless your thirst is desperate, don't drink straight from the bottle or can. Instead, use a glass or a beer mug, which allows the excess carbon dioxide to escape.

The trick is to gently pour most of the beer down the side of the slightly tilted glass or mug, with the last part poured down the middle to give the beer a full head and enhance its bouquet.

When serving home brew (or other bottle fermented brews), pour with great care to avoid any of the sediment getting into the glass. Here's how to do it:

❑ Line up the glasses and carefully remove the bottle cap.

❑ Tilt the first glass, then pour the beer slowly down the side, bringing the glass vertical as it fills up.

❑ Put down the full glass but keep the bottle tilted.

❑ Repeat with the other glasses until just before you reach the sediment, then stop.

Using the right glasses is an important part of running a home bar — and the first essential rule is never to use your beer glasses or mugs for anything other than beer. No matter how well you wash the glasses or mugs, foreign substances such as milk will stick to the glass and, even in minute quantities, will contaminate your beer, adversely affecting the taste.

When you wash your beer glasses, don't use detergent or soap. Instead, wash them in a very hot solution of baking soda or salt, then rinse in clean hot water. Don't use a cloth for washing or drying, but allow the mugs and glasses to air dry.

Experts say the ideal temperature for serving lager is 5.5°C; for all-malt beers 8°C to 10°C; for ale and Stout (including Guinness) 12.7°C.

But in the end your personal taste must determine the temperature at which you like your favourite brew. An ice-cold beer may sound good, but freezing it is one certain way to spoil a brew. When an all-malt beer is served below 7°C it will develop "chill haze"; this makes the beer hazy, but will usually clear when the temperature rises.

Why white froth?

A good head on the beer is a sure sign of an expert pourer, but have you ever wondered why the head and froth is white when the liquid's colour ranges from amber to black? *The Australian Brewers' Journal* supplied this answer way back in 1886:

This appears to be due to the reflection of the light from the outer surface of the several bubbles. When the surface is thus broken up, we have a cluster of little spheres, each of which presents a reflection to the eye from some part of its surface; and as there may be tens of thousands of these in a very small space, the effects become united, and are recognised as a whiteness.

But it may still be asked by some of us: how is it that the froth of a reddish liquid, such as beer, is white? The phenomenon of reflected light must again be appealed to for the means of solving this problem.

The colour of a liquid (not its froth) is determined by the transmitted light, not the reflected. If liquor be contained in a transparent glass vessel held between the eye and the light, and we look through it, the eye receives the light transmitted by the liquid, and deems the colour of that light to be the colour itself; but if we pour the liquor into an open vessel, and look obliquely at the surface, we shall find that the colour does not deviate much from whiteness, whatever the transmitted colour may be.

The liquid, whatever be its body-colour, is, when agitated, broken up into detached portions at its surface by the formation of bubbles, and each bubble reflects to the eye a portion of the light which falls upon it.

Consequently, if this reflected light is nearly white in all cases, the resulting assemblage of bubbles, generally known as froth, must always appear white, or nearly white.

What a way to have a beer!

Need an excuse to have a beer? Then why not blow your money — and get your mates to stage a "Bede-ale" to restore your fortune!

Bede-ale was a medieval male custom very much like the ancient concept of mateship. If an honest man suffered a financial setback, through no fault of his own, the law allowed his friends to drink him back to prosperity!

The publican, by law, had to hand over a certain percentage of all the money the drinkers spent during this Bede-ale session to the victim. The bigger the financial loss, of course, the longer — and drunker — the party. And, because it was permitted by law, no wife dared complain!

Other old customs involving beer drinking were

Bid-Ales, Bride-Ales, Give-Ales, Cuckoo-Ales, Help-Ales, Tithe-Ales, Leet-Ales, Lamb-Ales, Scot-Ales, Midsummer-Ales and Wedden-Ales.

Flip me a drop, please!

Flip, a very popular drink for our ancestors, is made this way, according to an old recipe:

Place in a saucepan one quart of strong ale together with lumps of sugar which have been well rubbed over the rind of a lemon, and a small piece of cinnamon.

Take the mixture off the fire when boiling and add one glass of cold ale.

Have ready in a jug the yolks of six or eight eggs well beaten up with powdered sugar and grated nutmeg.

Pour the hot ale from the saucepan on to the eggs, stirring them while so doing.

Have another jug at hand and pour the mixture as swiftly as possible from one vessel to the other until a white froth appears, when the flip is ready. One or two wine glasses of gin or rum are often added.

Here comes the bride — bearing beer

Bride-Ale was the English custom of the bride selling ale on her wedding day, for which she received any sum of money or present which her friends chose to give her.

And what parties those weddings were! One account from 1545 notes matter-of-factly: "When they came home from the church, then beginneth excesse of eatying and drynking, and as much is waisted in one daye as were sufficient for the two newe-married folkes half a yeare to lyve upon."

Egg on your mug

Egg Ale was a somewhat remarkable — and, on the face of it, a slightly revolting — concoction, although said to be highly nutritious. The old recipe stipulated:

To twelve gallons of ale was added the gravy of eight pounds of beef.

Twelve eggs, the gravy beef, a pound of raisins, oranges and spice, were then placed in a linen bag and left in the barrel until the ale had ceased fermenting.

Even then an addition was made in the shape of two

quarts of Malaga sack.

After three weeks in cask the ale was bottled, a little sugar being added.

Truly a monstrously potent drink!

A cock and beer story!

Ever tasted a Beer Cup? It certainly is a novel way to drink your beer — although few beer lovers today are likely to mix their favourite drink that way.

Popular at the beginning of the 18th Century, we read of Beer Cups with names like Humpty-dumpty, Clamber-clown, Hugmatee, Stick-back, Cock Ale and Knock-me-down.

Cock Ale, hailed as a "very strengthening and restorative compound", was made this way:

Take a cock of half a year old, kill him and truss him well, and put into a cask twelve gallons of Ale, to which add four pounds of raisins of the sun, well picked, stoned, washed and dried; sliced Dates, half a pound; nutmegs and mace two ounces.

Infuse the dates and spices in a quart of canary twenty-four hours, then boil the cock in a manner to a jelly, till a gallon of water is reduced to two quarts; then press the body of him extremely well, and put the liquor into the cask where the Ale is, with the spices and fruit, adding a few blades of mace.

Then put to it a pint of new Ale yeast, and let it work well for a day, and, in two days, you may broach it for use or, in hot weather, the second day; and if it proves too strong, you may add more plain Ale to palliate this restorative drink, which contributes much to the invigorating of nature.

These strange concoctions were served into small glasses from containers called posset pots — delicate glass bowls with one or two handles.

Dining and wining — all on beer!

Here's how to have your beer — and eat it! The monks of St. Francis of Paula, in Munich, in the 17th century started making a beer so "chewy" that it resembled "liquid bread" — and as such could be consumed during Lent.

Today the now secularised brewery, Paulanor Salvator, is the biggest in Munich and famous for its Double Bock.

And when is a beer called wine? When it's barley wine, of course. Strictly speaking, barley wine is an ale, not a beer. Traditionally, it is the strongest ale from a particular brewer and is sold in small bottles, known as "nips". It is best drunk from a wine glass.

Barley wine gets its high alcohol content from being left to mature for months in wooden casks, which are rolled over from time to time to stir the yeast into action to convert sugar into additional alcohol. The wood gives it a wine-like character.

Give us this day ...

Beer and religion were lucrative partners in the Middle Ages, when instead of holding a church bazaar, beer drinking binges by the entire congregation raised money for the parish.

Usually celebrated in a house called the Church House, these so-called Church-Ales were usually held on the birthday of the saint after whom a particular church was named, or whenever it was necessary to raise funds for repairs to the church or alms for the poor.

Actively encouraged by Pope Gregory, among others, profits from the large amounts of ale consumed did much to swell parish funds — and encourage a love for fundraising activities among parishioners.

As the Bishop of Bath and Wells reported to Archbishop Wells: "Church-Ales were when people went from afternoon prayers on Sundays to their lawful sports and pastimes in the churchyard, or in the neighbourhood, or in some public house, where they drank and made merry. By the benevolence of the people at these pastimes, many poor parishes have cast their bells and beautified their churches and raised stock for the poor."

Of course, they had wowsers even then, with one complaining that after a Church-Ale in Merrie Olde England "the people fell to lechery, and songs, and dances, with harping and piping, and also to gluttony and sin; and so turned their holiness to cursedness".

Oliver Cromwell finally banned Church-Ales and so ended a tradition that should have survived until today.

The early Finns loved their beer so much they even worshipped a god of beer called Pekko.

Protestant brew

Martin Luther was not only a reforming theologian — he was also such a great beer lover that a brewery used his picture to advertise its brew.

His favourite was Einbeck beer, brewed in Germany since 1351, which he loved so much the brewer gave him some as a gift for his wedding.

A well-known painting shows Luther being served with a huge jug of Einbeck beer during the Diet at Worms.

When Einbeck starting exporting bottled beer, they used a portrait of Luther to adorn the label.

A real bucketing

Ancient Saxon beer lovers drank their beer from their own personal ale-buckets — which were usually placed on their graves when they died.

Bloody marvellous!

David Ogilvy, advertising genius and one of the founders of the famous advertising agency Ogilvy and Mather, was brought up from the age of six on a diet of a bottle of beer to wash down a glassful of blood daily and calves brains three times a week.

As he recounts in his autobiography, *Blood, Brains and Beer*, the unusual diet was invented by his father, who believed it would make his son super-intelligent.

Beer cocktails:

Black velvet
Champagne and Guinness, usually mixed half-half, but quite enjoyable in whatever proportion you prefer. Mild.

Moscow Mule
Double shot of vodka in a beer glass topped up with beer. Very potent.

Beer heroes of history

Who was the greatest beer drinker in history? When it comes to free beers, there's no doubt the honour goes to Jedediah Buxton, who throughout his life meticulously tallied up every beer anyone had ever bought him since he started drinking — at the age of 12!

Sixty years or so later the total came to an amazing 5116 pints, equal to about 10,000 tinnies. Jedediah, an Englishman, claimed he could down a pint with only one breath — and won his free beers from those curious to see how many pints he could drink without losing his breath.

Thirsty Willie's grave problem

Beer certainly is healthy for you, but it can lead to a slight weight gain, as William Lewis discovered before his death in 1793.

His obituary tells how Thirsty Willie made it a rule, every morning of his life, to read a number of chapters in the Bible — and in the evening to drink eight gallons of ale.

"It is calculated," says one contemporary report, "that in his lifetime he must have drunk a sufficient quantity to float a seventy-four gun ship. His size was astonishing, and he averaged 40 stone.

"Although he died in his parlour, it was found necessary to construct a machine in the form of a crane, to lift his body in a carriage, and afterwards to have the machine to let him down into the grave."

Whether Willie left a bequest to buy the mourners a pint or two is not recorded.

Small beer — or is it?

Today, it's usual to dismiss an unimportant matter as "small beer". But where does the term come from?

It does not relate to a small quantity of beer, but to the weakest brew, which in Elizabethan times was called "small beer" (or, deprecatingly, "starve gut").

Strong beer, which cost more and was known as dragon's milk, merry-go-down or humming ale (from the way it made your head feel), was considered far more important to serious drinkers.

The expression *mind your p's and q's* also originated in Merrie Olde England where publicans served ale in pint or quart mugs.

If the customer was not careful, he could be charged for quarts (q's) when he had only been drinking pints (p's).

Champion Joe

When it comes to speedy drinking, Lancastrian Joe Johnson's gulping would be hard to beat. He regularly downed 80 pints of best bitter at his local pub — in a single night!

Some evenings he would gulp down five pints while the barman was ringing up the till.

As the 16-stone, red-faced beer lover's fame spread throughout Britain, challenges for beer drinking contests poured in from other would-be champion imbibers.

Two tough oil riggers from the North Sea fell down after 24-hours of solid drinking, leaving a disappointed Joe to keep going for another 12 hours on his own.

"I get this terrible thirst," Joe once explained. "There's no holding it back."

Golden rule for golden ale

In ancient Mesopotamia Queen Shu-Bad thought so highly of beer that she would drink it only one way — by sipping it through a straw made of solid gold.

Bountiful Bess's right royal treat

During the reign of Queen Elizabeth I, beer was divided into single beer, or small beer, double beer, double-double beer, and dagger ale, which was particularly sharp and strong.

Good Queen Bess, who served huge quantities of beer and ale at all royal functions, drank her own special royal brew which was said to be so strong that no one else in the household could handle it.

This little piggy went to the pub!

Have you ever pigged out on beer? Then you'll have some sympathy with the unfortunate porcines belonging to home-brewing parson Rev. John Woodforde in 1765, who wrote with some astonishment in his diary:

"Brewed a vessell of strong Beer today. My two large Piggs, by drinking some Beer grounds taken out of one of my Barrels today, got so amazingly drunk by it, that they were not able to stand and appeared like dead things almost, and so remained all night from dinner-time today. I never saw Piggs so drunk in my life, I slit their ears for them without feeling ..."

The next day the saga continued:

"My two Piggs are still unable to walk yet, but they are better than they were yesterday. They tumble about the yard and can be no means stand at all steady yet.

"Only this afternoon did they become tolerably sober ..."

How the rector fared after drinking the actual brew that produced such potent grains is not recorded. Although his handwriting for the week was decidedly shaky ...

Yuletide drinking

Good King Wenceslas of Christmas carol fame actually did exist — and he loved beer! The king ruled Bohemia in the 10th century and was so protective of the good beer brewed in his country that he passed a law forbidding the export of hop cuttings on pain of death.

Christmas also has a link with the strongest lager in the world, which is named after Santa Claus. Sam-

GARY COOPERS.

ichlaus (Santa Claus) beer, brewed specially for Christmas by the Swiss brewery Hurlimann, has an alcohol content of 11.2 by weight (14.9 by volume).

Amazingly, it is brewed only once a year, on December 6, which is St Nicholas (Santa Claus) day in Switzerland.

The lager is then left to mature and only released on December 6 of the following year. Interestingly, the same brewery makes the well-known non-alcoholic "beer" sold in supermarkets under the name Birrell.

The most potent beer in the world is Roger & Out, with 16.9% alcohol by volume and an original gravity of 1125°. It has been brewed at the Frog & Parrott in Sheffield, England, since 1985.

The strongest as measured by original gravity is The Doomsday Ale brewed by the Cornish Brewery Company with an alcohol content of 15.9% by volume and an original gravity of 1143.511°.

FLY Here often?!

Beer lover's bar quiz

Beer lovers should be authorities on their favourite drink — and what better way to impress your mates with your great knowledge than a quiz?

Particularly if, thanks to this book, you know all the answers (they appear on Page 162).

1. What Australian ale is related to a movie star?
2. What Elizabethan beer was known as "dragon's milk"?

3. What beer-based drink would you serve in a posset pot?

4. Who could regularly drink 80 pints of beer a night?

5. Why did a bride traditionally sell beer on her wedding day in Merrie Olde England?

6. In which icy country did people once baptise their children with ale?

7. What beer-related job did William Shakespeare's father perform with distinction?

8. What is the ideal temperature for serving lager?

9. What is "nux vomica", once used in beer?

10. In which country did a queen sip her beer through a straw made of solid gold?

11. Which country brews a beer at Christmas which is named after Santa Claus?

From barbie to banquet

There's no such thing as a free lunch, but Australasian pubs early this century certainly came close while catering for the culinary needs of their beer loving clientele.

In exchange for a threepenny glass of beer (or, more likely, six or seven glasses), one typical Melbourne pub laid on the following free fare daily, as reported in a 1911 edition of the *Australian Brewers' Journal*:

It is but 11 o'clock, yet biscuits and cheese, Fritz sausage, cold corned beef, salads, pickles, black and white puddings, and bread are spread out for the morning "supper".

At midday the regular lunchers begin to arrive. If they patronise the front or side bars they are welcomed by the appetising odour of hot pigs' cheek, in addition to the early morning menu.

In the back bars hot roasts or hot boiled joints are on the table. If the corned beef happens to be "on", carrots are served with it.

From midday until after 2 o'clock p.m. a barman stands behind the counter lunch table, and serves food out to the customers.

But that is not all. At 1 o'clock hot fried sausages and saveloys make their appearance, and, later in the afternoon, this is repeated. At certain times Welsh rarebit is served, and this kind of thing goes on until closing time at night.

The beer they served up in pubs those days was, by all reports, pretty potent, as an anonymous poet explained in the *Bulletin* in 1880:

Colonial Beer

A pot of beer, the beady bubbles breaking;
A hand outstretched to grab the pot and all;
An hour of jollity, a sad awakening;
An awful headache and a taste like gall.
An angry wife, in manner all unbending;
A voice, 'You're drunk', a stumble and a fall,
A Yankee broom upon your head descending,
And then you feel your wounds — and that is all.

Serving beer with meals

Certainly beer is the perfect drink for all occasions. For many, gulping down an ice-cold tinnie or two or three on a boiling day or around the barbie is the ultimate bliss.

Yet when the same people go out to dinner, chances are they'll become conventional and order a wine with their meal.

Beer is a great drink at the dinner table — and with almost every kind of food, as our ancestors knew only too well.

In many parts of Europe, particular the cold northern regions, people for centuries began and ended their days with beer.

As Michael Weiner points out in *The Taster's Guide to Beer*, the day began with "a good draught to wet your whistle; at the noonday meal a beer soup; and at supper, of course, there must be egg-flip made with beer.

"Raisin beer and sugar beer, fish and sausages boiled in beer, beer in all conceivable forms, to say nothing of abundant draughts of plain beer when paying visits, talking business, attending baptisms and funerals..."

England, too, had a great tradition of serving beer with food. The following charges appear in the household expenses of King Henry VIII:

The queen's maids of honour to have a chet loaf, a manchet, a gallon of ale, and a chine of beef for their breakfast. The brewer is informed not to put any hops or brimstone in the ale.

Today, lovers of barbecues and Asian foods know the golden brew enhances the taste of meat and spicy dishes.

But beer can compliment most other dishes as well. Just pick the correct brew and you can serve — and enjoy — beer with every course (except dessert, unless you are a real beer lover, that is!).

For **pre-dinner drinks**, offer your guests light, bitter, cold beer which will excite the gastric juices and work up an appetite.

Guinness goes down great with oysters served with brown bread, butter and lemon and with shellfish of every description.

For **main courses**, serve a strong, full-bodied beer (not too cold) with meat dishes and casseroles.

Curries also call for a full-bodied strong brew, but much colder. With spicy Oriental food, a sweetish, light to medium beer is the ideal companion.

Of course, if you're a true beer lover, you'll also want to cook with beer. The Vikings of old loved their beer so much they included a soup made of their favourite brew with every meal — and they ate six times a day!

A century ago beer mixed with brown sugar was a favourite sauce for pancakes; red herrings were steeped in small beer before being broiled; and catsup (the forerunner of today's ketchup) for sea stores was made mainly of beer and vinegar.

Here are a few tasty beer recipes to get you started:

Melon cocktail

Cut a large honeydew melon in half. Remove pips and scoop out balls. Place in a shallow dish and pour in beer until the melon balls are just covered. Stand for about 15 minutes, then put melon balls in cocktail glasses and cover them with chilled beer. Serves 6.

Beer soup

600ml beer
600ml milk
2 egg yolks, beaten
1 teaspoon butter
half teaspoon salt
1 dessert-spoon honey

Mix milk and beer, simmer for 15 minutes; add salt and honey; remove from heat and stir in butter and beaten egg yolks.

Beer Steak

500g rump steak
350ml beer
2 large onions
2 tablespoons butter
Salt and black pepper

Melt butter in shallow saucepan, add peeled and sliced onions and fry slowly until brown. Season steak, then place in saucepan on top of the onions. Cover and simmer on low heat for 90 minutes. Pour in the beer and continue simmering for two-and-a-half hours. Remove steak, thicken gravy with flour. Serve with mashed potatoes and vegetables.

Seafood-'n-beer casserole

250g prawns, cooked and shelled
250g tinned crab meat
4 cups beer
24 oysters
2 onions
4 shallots
1 stick of sliced celery
1 teaspoon parsley
50g butter
1 tablespoon flour
salt and pepper to taste

In shallow saucepan, bring to boil the beer, onions, parsley, celery and shallots. Simmer for 15 minutes. Season with salt and pepper. Add prawns, oysters and crab meat. Mix flour and butter into a paste, then add to the saucepan and stir until boiling. Serve with rice.

Beer bread

1 cup beer
250g plain flour
1 cup wholemeal flour
2 tablespoons caster sugar
15g yeast

Take a loaf tin 20x10x8cm and grease. Cream the yeast and sugar in a warmed basin until liquid. Bring beer to boil, then allow to cool until tepid. Stir the beer into the yeast, then add butter and continue stirring with wooden spoon to a smooth dough.

Brush with melted butter, then cover and leave in warm place until the dough doubles in size. Punch down.

Cover, wait until it doubles in size again. Punch down again, then shape into the tin and cover the top with melted butter. Leave in warm place until double in size, then bake in moderate oven (190°C, 375°F) for about one hour or until ready.

Ale and apple pie

600ml hot spiced ale
4 large cooking apples
2-3 tablespoons sugar
Grated peel of half lemon
Short pastry

Wash and core apples, then place them next to one another in a large pie dish. Mix butter, sugar and lemon peel into a firm paste. Pack into the cored hollows and smear surplus paste over the apple tops. Cover the dish with short pastry.

Bake in hot oven (250°C, 450°F) until pasty has risen. Lower to moderate (125°C, 350°F) and bake until pastry is brown. Carefully remove pastry without breaking.

Pour the hot spiced ale over the apples, cut the pastry into four and cover each apple with pastry. Serve with fresh cream.

Weird beer facts and feats

A letter by Pope Gregory to Archbishop Nidrosietisi, of Iceland, shows that in the 13th Century ale was so popular that some communities even used it to baptise their children! Wrote the boring old Pope: "... since the heart ought to be born again of water and the Holy Spirit, those ought not to be considered as duly baptised who have been baptised in ale."

On the other hand, when Pope Clement died, his last words betrayed his greatest love on earth: he asked for a beer.

Service with a five-headed smile

How's this for service? Barmaid Rosie Schedelbauer, carrying five full beersteins in each hand, dashed 15

metres to a world record in a mere four seconds in Germany.

And in England strongman Tommy Gaskin won himself a world record for raising a keg of beer weighing 62.5 kg above his head 656 times in only 6 hours.

Here's a job to thirst after

During the Middle Ages, being an official Ale Taster was a job many beer lovers clamoured for. And no wonder: you could drink officially all day, then get paid in beer!

Noted one writer in 1617: "John Shule had a patent from Arthur Lake, Bishop of Bath and Wells, and Vice-Chancellor of Oxford, for the office of ale-taster [to the University] and the making and assizing of barrels of beer.

"The office of ale tasting requires that he go to every ale-brewer that day they brew, according to their courses, and taste their ale; for which, his ancient fee is one gallon of strong ale and two gallons of small wort, worth a penny."

'Ale and hearty

Ancient Egyptian doctors believed fervently in the value of beer to treat every kind of disease (including, of course, the occasional hangover). Archeologists have found over 100 recorded medicines containing beer as the basic fluid.

Scientists at London's prestigious Guy's Hospital say beer helps to prevent dental caries. When teeth were soaked in a wide range of different solutions, those in the amber fluid remained perfect, while cavities appeared in the ones immersed in fruit juice.

Beer has sometimes been used as an aid in the diagnosis of disease, reported a scientist named Friedlander in a 1935 book titled *Successful Brewing*.

"It can be observed that with some people the foam from the beer immediately disappears and falls flat as they drink it," he noted.

"This phenomenon, often observed, may be explained by the fact that in such cases, the beer comes into contact with substances which increase the surface tension, whereby the foam holding capacity is destroyed.

"Diabetics often exhale acetone, diacetic acid, etc. Such powerful surface active substances overpower the relatively weaker foam stabilizers in beer and the foam collapses."

Can drinking beer cure the common cold? The

American Medical Society in 1958 reported the findings of ear, nose and throat specialist Dr Noah D. Fabricant:

"Beer (is) helpful in fighting the common cold — at least in the early stages. Although consumption of alcohol is obviously not a cure for the common cold, its beneficial role in some persons can neither be minimized or dismissed."

Royal truth

In 1436 a royal writ ordered the sheriffs of London to proclaim that "the drink called beere is a notable, healthy and temperate drink" — and anyone who said otherwise faced severe punishment.

You have my vote!

Ever dreamed of joining a political party whose sole reason for existing is to look after lovers of beer? Well, the Beer Lover's Party actually does exist — in Russia.

But when it tried to register as a political party, the 10,000 member organisation ran into trouble with vodka-loving officials of the Justice Ministry in Moscow.

"They said our name was too unusual for Russia," fumed Konstantin Kolachev, secretary-general of the Beer Lover's Party.

Instead, the ministry official suggested such titles as the "Sausage and Vodka Lover's Party", "People's Party for Democracy and Beer" ... even "Party of Lovers of Beer and Civic Accord"!

There were no takers for any of these — so the beer lovers abandoned politics and went back to steins.

THEY SNEAK UP ON YOU, YOU KNOW!

Strong beer!

In Czechoslovakia, beer is so good it keeps the currency afloat — literally! According to Michael Jackson in *The New World Guide to Beer*, in some small country breweries brewmasters show off the maturity of their beer in the lagering tank by placing a heavy coin on top of the foam, which is so dense that the coin does not sink.

Pilsener beer (sometimes also called Pilsner or Pils) derives its name from the Czech town of Pilsen, situated in the region still known as Bohemia. Hops has been grown in the region since the 9th century, indicating that brewing also took place there then.

Only in Germany

Almost 40 per cent of the world's breweries are in Germany — more than 1400 all told. And the Germans not only love their beer, but have many strange customs associated with the golden brew.

One is the tradition of drinking *Marzenbier* (literally, "March beer") in September. This goes back to the days when the last brew of the year was made at the onset of the hot weather in March, after which wild yeasts in the atmosphere would spoil any brew. This brew saw the thirsty Germans through the summer — and whatever was left was downed during a mighty party in September, when brewing resumed.

In parts of Germany a few centuries ago, anyone could sell beer — and many people had breweries in their cellars. When you were ready to brew for yourself or for sale, you bought your malt and hops, then contacted the village brewmaster who would turn up with all his equipment and help you brew the beer in the cellar.

Bock (literally, "goat") beer is a strong German brew and particularly popular in Bavaria, where the tapping of the first barrel of *Maibock* (a special Bock brewed in May, the most important season for this beer), is attended by the prime minister of the State and the mayor of Munich, the Bavarian capital.

Shocked and disgusted by the increase in the amount of coffee drunk by his subjects, Frederick the Great of Prussia in 1777 proclaimed:

"This must be prevented. My people must drink beer. His Majesty was brought up on beer and so were his ancestors, and his officers and soldiers."

Alas, 200 years later, coffee has become the most popular drink in Germany, with beer running second.

The first train to run in Germany, between Nuremberg and Furth in 1835, carried a typical German cargo — two barrels of beer.

Much Ado About Beer

William Shakespeare's father, John, was a man who knew his beer. In fact, he knew it so well that he was appointed an official ale-conner of his hometown, Stratford-on-Avon, in 1556.

The job of ale-conner was an important one, because it was he who tested the potency of beer, which by law had to be of at least a certain alcoholic strength before it could be sold.

Today, a hydrometer is used for the purpose, but John Shakespeare had to rely on his leather breeches to do the job. Like other ale-conners throughout the land, he would pour a pint of ale on a wooden stool in the pub attached to the brewery, then sit down in the pool for about 30 minutes, while downing a few pints to keep busy.

If the bar stool stuck to his leather breeches when he finally tried to get up, it meant the ale had failed the test and could not be sold, because it still had too much sugar and not enough alcohol.

On the other hand, if his breeches came free easily, it meant all the sugar in the ale had been converted to alcohol, producing a strong enough brew to satisfy the law — and the customers.

It's your shout!

The world's record "shout" took place in Langwarrin in 1894, when Major-General Tulloch shouted over 4000 soldiers to beer.

As beer lover Pat Lawlor recounts it in *The Froth Blower's Manual*, "The men filed into the canteen on one side, drank their beer and went out the other side.

It was a hot day so a few resourceful souls thought it a good idea to fall in again at the rear of the company.

"So an endless chain might have been set up but for the fact that after a while it developed slack and the General was saved from possible bankruptcy."

Hear the one about . . . ?

"The best colonial beer is made in Tasmania, whence it is shipped in frozen blocks to Australia and India," noted the 9th edition of the *Encyclopaedia Britannica*, under the entry for Brewing.

It continued: "In Calcutta on the hottest day, the residents now suck (not sip) their frozen pale ale." It was, of course, a hoax — pulled off by a disaffected staff member — which was discovered only after many copies had been sent out. Corrections were hurriedly made. The resale value of this edition skyrocketed.

Red beer

The first trademark ever registered in Britain and, it is claimed, in the world — was for beer! It was for the red triangle that identifies Bass Pale Ale even today.

Liquid cash

In 10th century Austria, cash flow and liquidity had a special meaning for the government — you could pay your taxes in either beer or wine!

All in a day's work

What a job for beer lovers! At Tasmania's famous Cascade Brewery, a reporter marvelled in 1894, a bell would ring at 3.50 for "beer time".

"Then work is suspended, and the hands all flock in with their billies, and each man has his pint of BAR-COO beer, which he drinks as he smokes until the bell rings again at 4 o'clock.

"The same programme takes place in the morning, and at midday and evening the men can each take home a pint of beer to their meals ... They all look well and hearty. There is one old man over seventy who takes his ale with the relish of youth."

In the 18th century, too, everyone drank beer — and lots of it. Benjamin Franklin noted that at one printing plant he knew, every worker drank a pint before breakfast, a pint with breakfast, a pint in mid-morning, another with lunch, a pint at six o'clock and another just before they finished work for the day. Most then headed for the nearest pub for a few more pints on the way home.

Devil's brew

The penalty for brewing a bad batch of beer could be serious indeed in Switzerland during the Middle Ages, when superstition all too often decreed that this was the fault of the Devil and that the brewster was a witch. The last "beer witch" was burned at the stake there in 1581.

Drinking for a good cause

When you down a Carlsberg, you're actually performing an act of cultural significance. Owned by the Carlsberg foundation, profits are used to support Danish art and science.

All at sea

When the US Navy's fast-attack submarine, *USS Pittsburgh*, was christened in 1984, a bottle of Iron City Beer, not champers, was used in the dedication ceremonies because beer was officially recognised as "an indigenous part of Pittsburgh".

Horsing around

In Norman times in England, during the king's travels through the country, the servants even washed the horses' feet in ale, much to the disgust of thirsty locals whose entire beer supply was sometimes used up for this purpose.

Drinking man's lament

Once, during Prohibition, I was forced to live for days on nothing but food and water.

— W.C. FIELDS

The fine art of beer tasting

Whether you've brewed it yourself, or paid out hard-earned cash over a bar, you'll have your own way of appreciating beer. But what exactly should you be looking for?

The sheer range of beers and refined flavours available means that what you should look for in one beer would be completely unacceptable in another. Bearing that in mind, a generalisation can be made.

First of all, the beer must look good. The colour should be what you are expecting: a Pilsner will be clear and golden, while a stout will be opaque and almost black. The head should be rich and creamy, deep and uneven.

Secondly, the bubbles should be small — large bubbles often indicate a beer that has not finished fermentation. And there should be no "bite" reflected in the overall taste from the carbonate.

An interwoven residue should be left on the glass as the beer retreats to the bottom. This is aptly, albeit somewhat romantically, termed "Brussels lace" by brewers.

Unless you are drinking a deliberately sedimented beer, it should be clear. Note that many beers contain sediment in the bottle, such as Coopers Sparkling Ale and many Belgian Trappist brews, but it should stay right there, in the bottle.

Skill is required in opening the bottle and pouring the beer without disturbing the sediment. German wheat beers, on the other hand, are meant to be served with a suspension of yeast.

The beer should have a distinctive aroma or "bouquet". This will be particular to the beer, but could be fruity, hoppy, herbal or malty.

How potent is that brew?

The number of methods of measuring the "strength" of a beer — both ancient and modern — are almost as plentiful as the types of beers they are used to measure.

The measurement methods fall into two main categories: by alcohol content and by density.

In countries such as the USA and Canada, beers are expressed in alcohol per cent by weight, or ABW. This produces a low number because the alcohol is "lighter" or less dense than water.

More usual is the measurement of alcohol per cent by volume, or ABV. This produces a slightly higher number for the same beer than the ABW.

For example, an American beer may contain 32g of alcohol in 1000g of beer. This would occupy, more or less, 40cl per litre. The ABW would be 3.2% and the ABV 4.0%.

Some traditional brewing nations, such as Britain, Germany and Belgium, prefer to measure the potency of their beer by density, reporting the Original Gravity or Degrees Plato. This is a product of history when brewers could predict — for taxation purposes — the amounts of each raw material they would use for the brewing process. How much of this material would turn into alcohol was harder to predict.

In a can, bottle or on tap?

The method of storing a beer can be almost as important as the way it is brewed in the first place.

With the exception of the sedimented beers, like many of the Belgians, beer is vulnerable to going off from the moment it leaves the brewery. Unlike a wine, a beer should not be "laid down" to mature.

A beer can "go off" in many ways, but the two most common are by reaction to light and oxidation. Exposure to strong light, such as in a supermarket, can cause a bottled beer to obtain a cabbagey taste and smell. Oxidation, by way of contact with the air, will cause a stale taste.

To overcome the above problems, always store your beers in a cool, but not cold, dark room or cellar — in the garage or under the stairs in most households. If it is in a bottle with a metal or plastic cap, store upright so the brew does not contact the cap.

If, however, the bottle is sealed with a cork, you should store it horizontally so the beer is in contact with the cork. This keeps the cork moist and prevents it contracting and allowing air in through the cracks.

Bad can

Should you buy beer in cans, bottles or on draught? As with all matters beer, this is not an easy question to answer. There is no firm evidence, but many brewers believe the prolonged contact of their beer with metal produces — wait for it — a metallic taste.

However, if you have just drunk a "bad can", it is more likely that a poor batch of beer has been produced and the brewers have sent it out in cans rather than through the trade.

This practice, although denied, does sometimes occur because cans are less likely to be returned than a draught beer in a pub or beer in a bottle — after all, it is the fault of the metal, isn't it?

Bottled beer is more likely to be pasteurised than draught beer, so the draught version will taste fresher. This, of course, is dependent on the publican rotating his stock correctly and keeping his lines clean.

Also, in a low turnover pub, the beer will suffer from lack of pasteurisation.

The final decision to be made, assuming you've opted for a draught beer, is should you have a large one or a small one, and should you take it in a straight glass or one with a handle?

If you are on a tasting session, it's probably better to stick with the small ones so your palate will remain more sensitive to differences — not to mention your head!

As to the shape of the glass, the main difference is likely to be your own preferences. However, it has been argued that a straight glass helps the carbonate evolve and move up the glass easier.

Recently, researchers from the University of Bristol, England, found that the shape of the glass plays an important role in helping you determine how much you drink.

In an experiment, 160 university students took almost twice as long to drink a beer in a straight-sided glass compared with a curved one.

Researcher Angela Attwood believes people drink quicker from curved glasses because it's harder to judge the halfway mark of your drink and therefore how much you've drunk.

Drinker's Calendar

366

Amazing, fun, bizarre, offbeat, odd, unusual, weird, staggering, stupendous, delightful true and invented reasons to have a drink every day of the year!

PLUS

How to say CHEERS!
around the world

JANUARY

1	2	3
New Year's Day.	Australia's first telephone exchange opened (1878).	Eskimos celebrate Blubber Day.
8	**9**	**10**
Newtown gets Aust.'s first Rugby League club (1908).	Yak Day in Outer Mongolia.	World's first underground railway opened in London (1863).
15	**16**	**17**
Sun worshippers holiday among Incas.	World's first full-sized saloon car exhibited (1903).	Aust.'s first ballet staged at Theatre Royal, Sydney (1835).
22	**23**	**24**
Sydney's first government trolley bus introduced (1934).	Humphrey Bogart's birthday.	Winston Churchill dies exactly 70 years after his father (1965).
29	**30**	**31**
Birthday of veteran drinker and hangover specialist W.C. Fields.	Another king loses his head, this time England's Charles I.	End of the first month of the new drinking year.

England: *Good health!* or *Cheerio!*

4	5	6	7
Siamese twins Masha and Dasha born in Russia (1950).	Edward the Confessor dies (1066).	England's King Richard II born (1367).	Aust.'s first recorded boxing match, in Sydney, over 56.
11	**12**	**13**	**14**
South Aust.'s first narrow-gauge railway opened	Railway line from Kalgoorlie to Leonora opened.	Thomas Crapper's self-raising toilet seat on display.	Queen Victoria uses the telephone for the first time (1878).
18	**19**	**20**	**21**
Movie star Cary Grant's birthday.	World's first women stockbrokers start in New York (1870).	King George V dies saying *Bugger Bognor* (1936).	Guillotine chops off the head of King Louis XVI (1793).
25	**26**	**27**	**28**
American gangster 'Scarface' Al Capone dies (1947).	Australia Day and Paul Newman's birthday.	Wolfgang Amadeus Mozart born.	Much married and lecherous King Henry VIII dies in his bed (1547).

Wales: *Jechyd d I chwi!* (Your health in drinking)

FEBRUARY

1 William Dean makes Aust.'s first balloon flight (1858).	**2** World's first public flushing loo opened in London (1852).	**3** Tequila Day in parts of Mexico.
8 Mary Queen of Scots loses her head (1587).	**9** Shoelace invented (1790).	**10** Queen Victoria's wedding anniversary.
15 Actor John Barrymore's birthday.	**16** Mule Day in the United States.	**17** Duke and Duchess of Gloucester visit Australia (1979).
22 First colour photo taken (1890).	**23** Drinking man and famous diarist Samuel Pepys' birthday.	**24** Nylon toothbrush bristles made (1938).
29 Leap year every fourth year.		

Italy: *Alla salute viva moi!*
(Good health — viva ourselves)

140

4	5	6	7
Rock star Alice Cooper's birthday.	Nose improver invented (1893).	Casanova eats 50 oysters for breakfast as aphrodisiac.	Military band gives Aust.'s first musical performance (1788).
11	**12**	**13**	**14**
Englishman Geo. Morgan world's first motorbike fatality (1899).	Abraham (Log Cabin) Lincoln's birthday.	Henry VIII's fifth wife loses her head (1542).	♥ Valentine's Day. ♥
18	**19**	**20**	**21**
World's first airmail flight, in India (1911).	Birthday of astronomer Nicolaus Copernicus.	Scotland's King James I dies in the loo (1437).	WWII RAF air ace Douglas Bader's birthday.
25	**26**	**27**	**28**
Opera singer Enrico Caruso's birthday.	First Aust. made car, a Pioneer, demonstrated (1897).	Convict Thos. Barrett first man hanged in Australia (1788).	Dunlop's first cycle tyre fitted (1888).

Scotland: *Slainthe eh — uit doch slainthe eh laut!*
(Hail to you — I leave you with a toast to your good
health) Sometimes abbreviated to *Slainthe!*

MARCH

1 David Niven's birthday.	**2** Spaniard finds rubber in South America (1530).	**3** Australia's first telegraph line opens to public (1854).
8 World's first game of snooker played, in India (1875).	**9** Russian space pioneer Yuri Gagarin's birthday.	**10** Australian patents first sheep shearing machine (1877).
15 Liz Taylor and Richard Burton's wedding anniversary.	**16** Slapstick king Jerry Lewis' birthday.	**17** St. Patrick's Day.
22 Explorer James Green eaten by cannibals (1766).	**23** Genghis Khan's birthday.	**24** Elvis Presley's first day in the US Army (1958).
29 Coca-Cola invented (1886).	**30** Painter Vincent van Gogh's birthday.	**31** Zip fastener patented (1896).

Netherlands: *Gezondheid!* (Good health)

4	5	6	7
World's first portrait photo studio opened in New York (1840).	Convict launches Aust.'s first newspaper (1803).	Michael-angelo's birthday.	Lassie's birthday.
11	**12**	**13**	**14**
World's first theatrical striptease in Paris (1893).	Irishman fails in bid to kill Prince Alfred in NSW (1867).	World's first reflecting road studs laid (1934).	Albert Einstein's birthday.
18	**19**	**20**	**21**
Houdini makes Australia's first powered flight (1910).	Victoria votes to introduce secret ballot at elections (1856).	Bear tried in Germany for terrorising villages (1499).	Birthday of composer Johann Sebastian Bach.
25	**26**	**27**	**28**
New Year's Day in England until 1751.	First artificial insemination on a dog (1885).	World's first traffic islands installed in Liverpool, UK, (1862).	Movie star Dirk Bogarde's birthday.

France: *A votre sante!* (To your health)
Also *Bon Sante!* (Good health)

A P R I L

1	2	3
April Fool's Day.	Cassanova's birthday.	Sydney gets Australia's first street lights (1826).
8	**9**	**10**
Bank of NSW becomes first bank to open in Australia (1817).	Roller skates first worn in public (1760).	Safety pin patented (1849).
15	**16**	**17**
Titanic strikes an iceberg and sinks (1912).	Charlie Chaplin's birthday.	Australia's first international exhibition opens in Sydney (1879).
22	**23**	**24**
Lenin's birthday.	Shakespeare's birthday.	Sydney gets Australia's first Post Office (1809).
29	**30**	
Jazz master Duke Ellington's birthday.	Hitler kills himself (1945).	

Switzerland: *Gsundtheit!* (Good health.

4	5	6	7
Ketch *Spitfire* becomes first Australian warship (1855).	Movie star Bette Davis' birthday.	Word *Telegram* coined (1852).	Matches invented (1688).
11	**12**	**13**	**14**
Convict James Bloodworth makes Aust.'s first bricks (1788).	First LPs produced (1904).	Gladiators first fight in Ancient Rome (264BC).	Abraham Lincoln assassinated (1865).
18	**19**	**20**	**21**
Scientists prove the top speed of a hare is 72 kph (1874).	British PM Benjamin Disraeli died (1881).	Adolf Hitler's birthday.	WW1 air ace the Red Baron shot down and killed (1918).
25	**26**	**27**	**28**
Anzac Day.	Queen's wedding anniversary.	S. American millipede found with 784 legs (1669.)	Mutiny on the *Bounty* (1789).

Sweden: *Skaal!* (Your health)
Also *Din skaal, min skaal, alla vackrajlickors skaal!*
(Your health, my health, the health of all pretty girls).

145

M A Y

1	2	3
Maypole dancing in Merrie Olde England.	Birthday of Russian Empress Catherine the Great.	Speed limit for steam cars set at 2 miles an hour (1864).
8	**9**	**10**
Philosopher Plato dies aged 81 (348BC).	World's first outboard motor produced (1896).	Fred Astaire's birthday.
15	**16**	**17**
First official Catholic Mass said in Australia by convict (1803).	Pianist Liberace's birthday.	First poodle parlour opened, in London (1896).
22	**23**	**24**
Sir Laurence Olivier's birthday.	First steam engine in Australia begins to grind wheat (1815).	Queen Victoria's birthday.
29	**30**	**31**
Bob Hope's birthday.	Australia's first dentist Simon Lear starts to yank out teeth (1818).	Brassiére invented (1914).

United States: *Here's to you!*

4	**5**	**6**	**7**
First motor hearse used, in New York (1900).	Napoleon Bonaparte dies (1851).	Sigmund Freud's and Rudolph Valentino's birthdays.	Gary Cooper's birthday.
11	**12**	**13**	**14**
World's first TV service starts (1928).	Florence Nightingale's birthday.	Birthday of heavyweight boxing champ Joe Louis.	World's first picture postcard engraved (1872).
18	**19**	**20**	**21**
Prima Ballerina Margot Fonteyn's birthday.	Nellie Melba's birthday.	Adelaide Cup Day.	Humphrey Bogart and Lauren Bacall's wedding anniversary.
25	**26**	**27**	**28**
Electric bed bug exterminator patented (1898).	Edmund Waller becomes MP aged 16 (1621).	Billiards invented (1591).	Harold Park hosts Australia's first greyhound race meeting.

Ireland: *Air do shlainte!* (Your good health)
Sometimes abbreviated to *Shlainte!*

JUNE

1	2	3
Marilyn Monroe's birthday.	Queen Elizabeth's coronation (1953).	Composer George Bizet dies (1875).
8	**9**	**10**
France's Louis XIV introduces high-heeled shoes (1668).	Nero commits suicide (AD68).	Ball-point pen patented (1943).
15	**16**	**17**
Benjamin Franklin discovers electricity (1752).	World's first public address system used (1913).	First magazine to publish a photograph (1846).
22	**23**	**24**
Australia's first test tube baby born in Melbourne (1980).	King Edward VIII's birthday.	Grand Prix ace Juan Fangio's birthday.
29	**30**	
William Hart wins first air race held in Australia (1912).	Last day of the first half of the year.	

Chinese: *Gan bei* (Dry the cup)

4	5	6	7
Recruting Officer is first play staged in Australia (1789).	Robert Kennedy gunned down (1968).	Tennis ace Bjorn Bjorg's birthday.	Painter Paul Gaugin's birthday.
11	**12**	**13**	**14**
Grand Prix ace Jackie Stewart's birthday.	US student throws playing card 56.4 metres (1979).	Alexander the Great dies from over eating (323BC).	British horse population reaches 3.5 million (1902).
18	**19**	**20**	**21**
Wellington wins Battle of Waterloo (1815).	Book matches invented in USA (1892).	Tasmanian boozer and movie star Errol Flynn's birthday.	Film actress Jane Russell's birthday.
25	**26**	**27**	**28**
Custer's Last Stand (1876).	Fat, drunk King George IV dies from over-indulgence (1830).	Philosophical Society of Australasia founded (1821).	Coronation of Queen Victoria (1838).

Czech: *Na zdraví* (To your health)

JULY

1	2	3
Aviatrix Amy Johnson takes off from UK for Australia (1903).	Boozer and author Ernest Hemingway shoots himself (1961).	Cigarette lighter invented (1816).
8	**9**	**10**
World's first supermarket open in USA (1912).	Doughnut patented (1872).	Engagement of Princess Elizabeth to Prince Philip (1947).
15	**16**	**17**
Flush toilet invented (1589).	First airmail from Melbourne to Sydney (1914).	James Cagney's birthday.
22	**23**	**24**
Chi Chi the panda died (1972).	Tulip Day in parts of Holland.	N. Howse wins Australia's first VC (1900).
29	**30**	**31**
Mussolini's birthday.	Henry Ford's birthday.	Cat Day in Spain.

Arabic: *Fisehatak* (To your health)

4	5	6	7
Gina Lollobrigida's birthday.	Aust.'s first agricultural society founded (1822).	Russian Tsar Nicholas I's birthday.	Beetle Ringo Starr's birthday.
11	**12**	**13**	**14**
Yul Brynner's birthday.	Julius Caesar's birthday.	Vacuum cleaner invented (1901).	Billy The Kid shot dead (1881).
18	**19**	**20**	**21**
Cricket legend W.G.Grace's birthday.	Count Dracula claims his first victim (1587).	Plastic invented (1866).	Poet Robert Burns' birthday.
25	**26**	**27**	**28**
First flight over the English Channel (1909).	Rock star Mick Jagger's birthday.	Manhatten cocktail invented (1928).	Jackie Kennedy Onnassis' birthday.

Greenlandic: *Kassutta* (Let our glasses meet)

A U G U S T

1	2	3
First pillar boxes for mail (1849).	Donkey Day in Ethiopia.	Pencil eraser invented (1770).
8	**9**	**10**
Great Train Robbery (1963).	Exclamation mark invented (1553).	First dahlia show in Perth (1877).
15	**16**	**17**
Napoleon's birthday.	First department store opens (1848).	Davy Crockett's birthday.
22	**23**	**24**
First movie show in Australia (1896).	Rudolf Valentino died (1926).	First woman jockey, in England (1804).
29	**30**	**31**
Australia wins Ashes first time (1882).	Drinking chocolate invented (1656).	Jack the Ripper strikes (1888).

Afrikaans: *Gesondheid* (To your health)

4	5	6	7
Birthday of poet Percy Bysshe Shelley.	Film actor Robert Taylor's birthday.	Robert Mitchum's birthday.	First Aussie Rules match played, in Melbourne (1858).
11	**12**	**13**	**14**
Dish-washing machine invented (1889).	King George IV's birthday.	Alfred Hitchcock's birthday.	First soccer match in Australia, in Sydney (1880).
18	**19**	**20**	**21**
Elvis Presley buried (1977).	Aerial pioneer Orville Wright's birthday.	Aztecs celebrate Moon's birthday.	World's first film festival ends (1932).
25	**26**	**27**	**28**
Aust.'s first church building opened (1793).	Cleopatra's birthday.	Vulcanic island Krakatoa exploded (1883).	Goat's Day in Mali.

Swahili: *Maisha marefu* (Good life)

SEPTEMBER

1 First railway carriage with a flush toilet (1859).	**2** Great Fire of London (1666).	**3** Actor Alan Ladd's birthday.
8 First fully automatic totalisator in Australia (1917).	**9** Fire extinguisher invented (1743).	**10** First circus (1769)
15 Agatha Christie's birthday.	**16** First TV service starts in Australia (1956).	**17** Coin gas meter patented (1887).
22 First radio message direct from UK to Aust. received (1918).	**23** Mickey Rooney's birthday.	**24** Ice cream first served (1686).
29 World's first cops go on the beat in London (1829).	**30** Jack The Ripper strikes twice (1888).	

Australian: *Cheers mate!*

4	5	6	7
Roll-film camera patented (1888).	First petrol pump delivered (1885).	First cigarettes made commercially (1843).	Birthday of Queen Elizabeth I.
11	**12**	**13**	**14**
World's first TV play (1928).	First steam railway opened in Australia (1854).	Superman's birthday.	Football pools launched in UK (1922).
18	**19**	**20**	**21**
Greta Garbo's birthday.	Carpet sweeper patented (1876).	Sofia Loren's birthday.	First gift coupons introduced, by New York shop (1865).
25	**26**	**27**	**28**
IQ test devised (1905).	Liner *Queen Mary* launched (1934).	Liner *Queen Elizabeth* launched (1938).	Brigitte Bardot's birthday.

Estonian: *Terviseks* (For the health)

OCTOBER

1 Julie Andrews' birthday.	**2** Australia's first bridge, in Sydney (1788).	**3** Jelly babies invented (1870).
8 First photocopier marketed (1907).	**9** Beetle John Lennon's birthday.	**10** Potato crisps first made (1853).
15 First reported horse race meeting in Australia (1810).	**16** Oscar Wilde's birthday.	**17** Stuntman Evel Knievel's birthday.
22 Captain Cook meets King of Tonga (1773).	**23** First heart transplant in Australia (1968).	**24** World's first plastic surgery (1814).
29 Twins Day in Nigeria.	**30** First daily newspaper comic strip (1904).	**31** Halloween.

Latvian: *Priekā* (To joy)

4	5	6	7
Silent screen star Buster Keaton's birthday.	Picture postcard introduced (1872).	First talkie movie *The Jazz Singer* released (1927).	Motorcycle cops take to the road, in New York (1905).
11	**12**	**13**	**14**
Adding machine patented (1887).	Columbus discovers America (1492).	First paperback book published (1841).	Battle of Hastings (1066).
18	**19**	**20**	**21**
Cocoa first sold (1828).	Poet Adam Lindsay Gordon's birthday.	Jackie Kennedy marries Onassis (1968).	Edison invents light bulb (1879).
25	**26**	**27**	**28**
Al Capone's second day in jail (1931).	Actor Jackie Coogan's birthday.	Boozer and poet Dylan Thomas' birthday.	Captain James Cook's birthday.

Maori: *Mauri ora* (To life)

N O V E M B E R

1	2	3
Michael-angelo finishes Sistine Chapel ceiling (1512).	First scheduled Qantas flight (1922).	Independence Day in Panama.
8	**9**	**10**
Birthday of Dracula's creator Bram Stoker.	Australia's first naval victory, by HMAS *Sydney* (1914).	Stanley meets Livingstone (1871).
15	**16**	**17**
First rubberised raincoat (1747).	Hottentots celebreate Feast of the Baboon.	Suez Canal opened (1869).
22	**23**	**24**
John F. Kennedy assassinated (1963).	2BL becomes Australia's first radio station (1923).	First jukebox installed (1889)
29	**30**	
First Holden produced (1948).	Winston Churchill's birthday.	

Romanian: *Noroc* (Good luck)

4	5	6	7
Machine gun patented (1862).	Guy Fawkes' Day.	Motor car bumpers patented (1905).	Marie Curie's birthday.
11	**12**	**13**	**14**
Ned Kelly hanged (1880).	Grace Kelly's birthday.	Bra patented in USA (1914).	Prince Charles' birthday.
18	**19**	**20**	**21**
Scooter invented (1897).	First newspaper colour supplement (1893).	Queen Elizabeth's wedding anniversary.	First submarine, built from wood and skins (1624).
25	**26**	**27**	**28**
Premiere of *The Mousetrap* (1952).	First table tennis sets made (1898).	World's first one-way streets, in London (1617).	Beer shandy invented (1847).

Turkish: *Şerefe* (To honour)

159

D E C E M B E R

1 World's first Labour government, in Queensland (1899).	**2** Neon lighting introduced (1910).	**3** First heart transplant (1967).
8 Australia's first parachute jump, from a balloon (1888).	**9** Kirk Douglas' birthday.	**10** Nobel Prize established (1896).
15 First building regulations in Australia (1810).	**16** Boston Tea Party (1773).	**17** Wright brothers fly (1903).
22 Angora Goat Day in Namibia.	**23** Swazi Queen Great She Elephant's birthday.	**24** Pre-Christmas drinks.
29 First animated cartoon (1906).	**30** Fountain pen invented (1656).	**31** Hogmanay.

Hebrew: *L'Chayyim* (To life)

4	5	6	7
Emperor Bokassa crowned (1977).	First glider flight in Australia (1909)	Edison invents phonograph (1877).	Encyclopaedia Britannica launched (1768).
11	**12**	**13**	**14**
World's first municipal park (1834).	Shane Gould sets 1500m freestyle record (1971).	World's first motor show (1894).	Queen Victoria's husband died (1861).
18	**19**	**20**	**21**
SA gives women vote, first in Australia (1894).	Christmas crackers invented (1861).	Sir Robert Menzies' birthday.	World's first crossword published (1913).
25	**26**	**27**	**28**
Christmas Day.	Boxing Day.	Peter Pan born on stage (1904).	Chewing gum patented (1869).

Bulgarian: *Nazdrave* (To health)

"I bet you don't know this" answers

1. Page 47
2. Page 78
3. Page 35
4. Page 51
5. Page 75
6. Page 65
7. Page 139
8. Page 41
9. Page 61
10. Page 59

11. Page 72
12. Page 68
13. Page 19, 24
14. Page 617
15. Page 11
16. Page 67
17. Page 53
18. Page 63
19. Page 65
20. Page 13

Beer Lover's Bar Quiz answers

1. Page 133
2. Page 108
3. Page 104
4. Page 109
5. Page 102
6. Page 122

7. Page 128
8. Page 98
9. Page 88
10. Page 110
11. Page 111

www.ingramcontent.com/pod-product-compliance
Lightning Source LLC
Chambersburg PA
CBHW060928040426
42445CB00011B/851